MENTAL HEALTH & AGING

Michael A. Smyer, PhD, is a Professor of Human Development at The Pennsylvania State University. He has published extensively on a broad range of research interests and policy concerns, which include the effects of mental health interventions in nursing homes, notions of health and well-being for older adults and families, the problems of workers in long-term care, and the effects of pharmaceutical assistance programs for elders. He is the recent recipient of Penn State's Pattishall Award for Outstanding Research Achievement and numerous other professional honors. After receiving his undergraduate degree from Yale, he was working on his doctorate in clinical psychology at Duke University when he was presented with the opportunity to evaluate a therapy program for older adults, and his interest seemed to gel. After receiving his doctorate, Smyer was hired to do applied gerontology at Penn State and established a clinical practice. He also received an American Council on Education Fellowship in Academic Administration and served as Associate Chairman of Penn State's Gerontology Center and Professor-in-Charge of the University's Department of Individual and Family Studies.

MENTAL HEALTH & AGING

PROGRESS & PROSPECTS

MICHAEL A. SMYER, PhD
EDITOR

Originally published as the Winter/Spring 1993 issue of *Generations*,
Journal of the American Society on Aging, Mary Johnson, Editor

SPRINGER PUBLISHING COMPANY
NEW YORK

Copyright © 1993 by Springer Publishing Company, Inc.

Cover and interior design by Holly Block

Springer Publishing Company, Inc.
536 Broadway
New York, NY 10012-3955

Second Printing
98 99 00 / 5 4 3 2

Library of Congress Cataloging-in-Publication Data

Mental health and aging: progress and prospects / Michael
    Smyer, editor.
        p. cm.
        Contains reprinted articles from <u>Generations</u> issued by
American Society of Aging.
        Includes bibliographical references and index.
        ISBN 0-8261-8380-8
        1. Aged—Mental health. 2. Geriatric psychiatry.
    3. Aged—Mental health services—United States.   I. Smyer,
    Michael A.
    II. Generations
        [DNLM: 1. Mental Health—in old age—collected works. 2.
    Aging–physiology—collected works. 3. Health Services for
    the Aged. WT150 M5492 1993]
    RC451.4. A5M4342 1993
    618.97'689—dc20
    DNLM/DLC
    for Library of Congress   93-32953
                                                                                  CIP

Printed in the United States of America

This book was typeset at Springer Publishing Company using 10.5/14 pt. Adobe New Baskerville with Macintosh hardware and *Quark Xpress* software.

Contents

Contributors

Jerry Avorn, MD, is Associate Professor of Medicine, Harvard Medical School, and Director of the Program for the Analysis of Clinical Strategies, Gerontology Division, Brigham and Women's Hospital, Boston.

Mindy J. Blum, PhD, is a Postdoctoral Fellow in HIV Psychosocial Services, Department of Psychiatry, Harbor-UCLA Medical Center, Torrance, CA.

Sandra L. Boyd-Davis, PhD, is a Research Analyst, Southern California Regional Headquarters, Kaiser Permanente Health Plan Organization, Pasadena, CA.

Gene Cohen, MD, PhD, is Acting Director, National Institute on Aging, National Institutes of Health, Bethesda, MD.

Marian Cleeves Diamond, PhD, is Professor, Department of Integrative Biology, and Director, Lawrence Hall of Science, University of California, Berkeley.

Marilyn Engstrom, RN, MSN, CS, is Coordinator in the Gerontology Program, New Jersey State Department of Health, Trenton.

Sanford I. Finkel, MD, is Director, Gero-Psychiatric Services, Northwestern University Medical School, Chicago.

Margaret Gatz, PhD, is a Professor of Psychology, University of Southern California, and a Senior Research Associate, Ethel Percy Andrus Gerontology Center, University of Southern California, Los Angeles.

Linda K. George, PhD, is Professor in the Departments of Psychiatry and Sociology at Duke University, Durham, NC, where she also serves as Associate Director of the Center for the Study of Aging and Human Development.

Robert Goisman, MD, is Instructor in Psychiatry, Harvard Medical School, and Director, Outpatient Training and Research, Massachusetts Mental Health Center, Boston.

Rickey Greene, MSW, is Program Manager in the Gerontology Program, New Jersey State Department of Health, Trenton.

Bennett Gurian, MD, is Associate Professor of Psychiatry, Harvard Medical School, and Senior Consultant in Geropsychiatry, New England Deaconess Hospital, Boston.

Jerry H. Gurwitz, MD, is Instructor in Medicine, Harvard Medical School, and member of the Program for the Analysis of Clinical Strategies, Gerontology Division, Brigham and Women's Hospital, Boston.

Helen Q. Kivnick, PhD, is Associate Professor, School of Social Work, University of Minnesota, Minneapolis.

Bob G. Knight, PhD, is the Merle H. Bensinger Associate Professor of Gerontology and Psychology at the Andrus Gerontology Center, University of Southern California, Los Angeles, and serves as Director of the Andrus Older Adult Center and the Los Angeles Caregiver Resource Center.

Barry D. Lebowitz, PhD, is Chief of the Mental Disorders of the Aging Research Branch, National Institute of Mental Health.

Claude A. Mellins, PhD, is a Postdoctoral Research Fellow at the HIV Center for Clinical and Behavioral Studies, Columbia University, New York State Psychiatric Institute, New York City.

Mark Monane, MD, MS, is Instructor in Medicine, Harvard Medical School, and a member of the Program for the Analysis of Clinical Strategies, Gerontology Division, Brigham and Women's Hospital, Boston.

Carol M. Musil, PhD, RN, is a Post-doctoral Fellow in geriatric mental health nursing at Case Western Reserve University, Cleveland, OH.

Sara Honn Qualls, PhD, is Associate Professor of Psychology, Director of the Center on Aging, and Director of Clinical Training, University of Colorado at Colorado Springs.

Mary Casey O'Connor, MSW, ACSW, is Public Health Consultant, Social Work, in the Gerontology Program, New Jersey State Department of Health, Trenton.

Larry D. Rickards, PhD, is the Assistant Director of the National Association of Area Agencies on Aging, Washington, DC, and Chair of the Coalition on Mental Health and Aging.

Edmund Sherman, PhD, is Professor, School of Social Welfare, and Faculty Research Associate, Ringel Institute of Gerontology, State University of Albany.

Candace Stacey-Konnert, PhD, is an Assistant Professor, Department of Psychology, University of Calgary, Alberta, Canada.

Larry Tune, MD, MAS, is Associate Professor, Department of Psychiatry and Behavioral Sciences, and Director, Dementia Research Clinic, The John Hopkins Hospital, Baltimore, MD.

Terrie Wetle, PhD, is the Director of the Braceland Center for Mental Health and Aging at the Institute of Living, a large psychiatric hospital and service system in Hartford, CT, and Associate Professor of Community Medicine and Health Care at the University of Connecticut School of Medicine, and Director of the Research Curriculum for the Travelers Center on Aging.

May L. Wykle, PhD, RN, FAAN, is Florence Cellar Professor, Chairperson for Gerontological Nursing, Associate Dean for Community Affairs, and Director of the Center on Aging and Health, Case Western Reserve University, Cleveland, OH.

Introduction

Mental Health and Aging:
Progress and Prospects

The chapters in this volume are designed to highlight the
progress and prospects of a vibrant field. We can be illustrative here because of other more extensive treatments of
the field (e.g., Birren, Sloane and Cohen, 1992; Butler,
Lewis and Sunderland, 1991), as well as fuller discussions of specific
disorders (e.g., Light and Lebowitz, 1990; Miller and Cohen, 1987;
Salzman and Lebowitz, 1991) and of the processes of mental health in
later life (e.g., Baltes and Baltes, 1990; Erikson, Erikson and Kivnick,
1986; Sherman, 1991).

This collection provides a snapshot from a kaleidoscope of activity
in research and clinical practice in mental health and aging. Like a
snapshot, it cannot be comprehensive. It emphasizes certain aspects of
the activities, blurs others, and completely excludes yet others. The
hope, however, is that the depiction can convey a sense of the field—a
sense of the excitement, the progress, and the challenges that remain.

Several themes formed the foundation for this collection. First, it
was important to provide a context for current clinical and practice
efforts. Second, it was important to highlight both the progress made
and the areas of continuing challenge. Finally, it was important to
reflect the complexity of the field: Mental health and aging is a function of individual, familial, and societal elements.

Throughout this volume we will confront the paradoxes of this field of research and practice:

- Not all elderly are mentally ill; so, too, not all elderly are mentally healthy—"vitally involved" in Helen Kivnick's phrase.
- We have made a great deal of progress, as Sandy Finkel reports. However, there are still major challenges in basic elements, such as accurately depicting the phenomenology of depression in later life, as Linda George points out.
- We have a richer understanding of the complexity of population patterns of mental illness and health, as May Wykle and Carol Musil point out. But we still struggle to understand the richness and complexity of the individual life, as Gene Cohen portrays in his chapter.
- We are painfully aware of the debilitating effects of mental illness, particularly cognitive impairment, as Claude Mellins and her colleagues report. Yet we are also excited by Marian Diamond's findings on the plasticity of cognitive functioning, even very late in life.
- We must accurately assess the debilities and inadequacies of older adults who need care, but we also know that optimal treatments will engage the strengths, as well as weaknesses, of older adults, as Sherman, Cohen, Kivnick, and Knight point out.
- We are focused on the priorities of older adults and an aging society. But Barry Lebowitz reminds us that we have to see our concerns within the larger framework of a federal system struggling with issues of access, quality, and cost-containment. Of course, these issues are not limited to the governmental sector, as Terrie Wetle reminds us.
- Mental health and aging concerns are at once high tech and high touch. From Larry Tune's fine review of neuroimaging techniques to Mark Monane and colleagues' discussion of pharmacotherapy in long-term care—it is clear that we are seeing the benefits of increasing sophistication in the application of advanced technologies to the mental health challenges of later life. At the same time, however, effective therapeutic work requires close working with older adults and their families, as many of our contributors point out (e.g., Gurian and Goisman, Knight, Sherman, Qualls).

If successful, we will convey both the progress that has been made in this field, and the challenges that remain for continuing research and practice.

MICHAEL A. SMYER

References

Baltes, P. and Baltes, M. M., eds., 1990. *Successful Aging: Perspectives from the Behavioral Sciences.* New York: Cambridge University Press.

Birren, J. E., Sloane, R. B. and Cohen, G. D., eds., 1992. *Handbook of Mental Health and Aging, 2nd ed.* San Diego, CA: Academic Press, pp. 721–62.

Butler, R. N., Lewis, M. and Sunderland, T., 1991. *Aging and Mental Health: Positive Psychosocial and Biomedical Approaches, 4th ed.* New York: Merrill.

Erikson, E. H., Erikson, J. M. and Kivnick, H. Q., 1986. *Vital Involvement in Old Age.* New York: Norton.

Light, E. and Lebowitz, B. D., eds., 1990. *Alzheimer's Disease: Treatment and Family Stress.* New York: Hemisphere.

Miller, N. E. and Cohen, G. D., eds., 1987. *Schizophrenia and Aging.* New York: The Guilford Press.

Salzman, C. and Lebowitz, B. D., eds., 1991. *Anxiety in the Elderly.* New York: Springer Publishing Company.

Sherman, E., 1991. *Reminiscence and the Self in Old Age.* New York: Springer Publishing Company.

MENTAL HEALTH

&

AGING

Mental Health of Older Persons
Social and Cultural Factors

May L. Wykle and Carol M. Musil

learly, mental health has come of age and is central to the current health promotion emphasis with older adults. Gerontologists interested in the continued development and well-being of aged persons must focus on the mental health of older adults, once a neglected issue. As they do so, their perspectives on mental health and aging must integrate the separate and combined influences of developmental tasks with life-span contexts and trajectories (Baltese, Reese and Lipsitt, 1980; Wykle and Musil, in press). As people age, there is increasing diversity and heterogeneity. Biological, psychological, and sociocultural factors, combined with individual and family expectations, act as multiple determinants of mental health adjustment in old age. Therefore, it is important to specify the effects of social and cultural influences on the mental health of older adults, particularly as their numbers increase.

This chapter is designed to focus attention on the intersection of psychosocial and sociocultural factors as they affect older adults' experience of mental health and mental illness in later life. The first part will provide a brief overview of the epidemiology of mental illness across the life span, with some attention to treatment patterns for older adults. The next part considers the social and cultural correlates of mental health problems among older adults. The final part considers the practice implications of the diversity of influences on older adults' mental health. Throughout this chapter, two themes are emphasized: the heterogeneity of influences on older adults' mental well-being, and the dearth of research on the interacting roles of multiple influences on older adults' mental health.

EPIDEMIOLOGIC PERSPECTIVES

Life-Span Patterns

Mental illness occurs less frequently in older adults than in younger persons, and some psychiatric symptoms that affect older persons differ from those experienced by the young. Older adults of both genders have lower rates of affective, anxiety, and substance use disorders, but higher rates of severe cognitive impairment (Regier et al., 1988). Cognitive impairment increases with age and, according to the Epidemiologic Catchment Area (ECA) Program data, is estimated to be 2.9 percent for those aged 65–74, 6.8 percent for those 75–84 years old, and 15.8 percent for those over 85 years (Regier et al., 1988). Approximately 4.2 percent of men are likely to experience cognitive impairment between the ages of 65–74 compared to 1.9 percent of women the same age.

The clinical manifestations of mental health problems in older adults may vary from those of younger persons. The most frequently studied indicators of the psychological status of elders are depression and life satisfaction, even though anxiety disorders are twice as prevalent (Regier et al., 1988). Data from the five ECA Program sites indicate that anxiety disorders affect 5.5 percent of those over age 65 (Regier et al., 1988), but these disorders have received less attention than other syndromes until recently (Rabins, 1992). Across the life span, only substance use disorders in males aged 18–44, affective disorders in women 25 to 64, and severe cognitive impairment in those 75 years and older are more prevalent than anxiety disorders. The most frequent cognitive disorders in the elderly include multi-infarct dementia, Alzheimer's disease, and delirium (Rabins, 1992). The prevalence of multi-infarct dementia might decrease in the future as individuals control diet and blood pressure, exercise, and receive treatment for cardiac problems. Interestingly, older adults' participation in positive health behaviors may be related to socioeconomic factors

(House et al., 1992) that influence strategies used to promote health.

A significant number of older adults experience some degree of depression, with the largest proportion being mildly affected. The incidence of major or minor depression among nursing home residents is estimated to be 15–25 percent (National Institutes of Health, 1991). According to the ECA data (Regier et al., 1988), approximately 2.5 percent of older adults experience affective disorders, specifically major depression (0.7%) and dysthymia (1.8%).

Based on data from the Piedmont ECA site, Blazer, Hughes, and George (1987) reported that while only a small number of subjects had clinical depression or dysthymia, approximately 15 percent of the sample experienced some dysphoric symptoms that did not meet the criteria for affective disorder. Given the extent of depressive symptomatology among older persons in contrast to the relatively low rates of diagnosed clinical depressions, the prevalence of depressed mood in older adults may be underestimated (Blazer, Hughes and George, 1987). The relationship between the presence of symptoms and the need for treatment is not well delineated (Bebbington, 1990), nor are the effects of dysphoria on lifestyle and functioning in old age well documented. These effects can be expected to range from subtle to pronounced. Older persons commit 17 percent of all suicides (Koenig and Blazer, 1992). Indeed, suicide has become one of the leading causes of death among older persons, particularly elderly white males and those suffering from chronic illness or pain (Wykle, Segal and Nagley, 1992). Frequently elderly depressed persons who are suicidal consult a physician about their physical health (Rabins, 1992) rather than their mental status.

Treatment Patterns

Despite these lifetime prevalence patterns, treatment for psychiatric symptoms of older adults has lagged because a vast majority of people believe that mental health decline is inevitable with aging. In a study of 1,300 elders, Haug, Belgrave, and Gratton (1984) found that while some subjects showed a decline in mental health and an increase in psychiatric symptoms over the course of a year, approximately 70 percent stayed the same or improved. Most older persons maintain a satisfactory level of mental health, but for those who do experience changes in their psychological status, appropriate and accessible treatment is essential.

The recognition and treatment of the mental health problems of older Americans remain a challenge. Older persons are less likely than younger adults to seek treatment for mental health problems through formal mental health care systems. While it is estimated that approximately 7.8 percent of all community-residing elders have a need for psychiatric services, only 2.5 percent of older persons in the community receive treatment from mental health professionals, and another 2.4 percent obtain care from their primary physician (Burns and Taub, 1990). Thus, a substantial number of older adults who might benefit from mental health treatment are not receiving care from either sector. Primary care providers are likely to remain the major source of identification, treatment, and referral for psychiatric problems in current cohorts of elderly. This pattern may change as today's younger adults, who are somewhat more likely to seek mental health care from a specialist, advance to old age (Gatz and Smyer, 1992).

A number of older adults with mental health disorders receive institutional care either in psychiatric hospitals or in nursing homes. It is estimated that between 43 to 60 percent of those admitted to nursing homes have some type of mental disorder (Gatz and Smyer, 1992). Depression, anxiety, confusion, and paranoia are among the most frequent reasons for admission of an elderly person to a psychiatric hospital. In a study of 152 elderly psychiatric inpatients, 63 percent were admitted for depression, 34 percent for agitation, and 31 percent for confusion. A smaller percentage of those admitted experienced symptoms of alcohol and drug abuse or had delusional ideation (Nagley et al., 1988). Older adults who are institutionalized for psychiatric care are likely to present with multiple symptoms and problems, including concomitant physical illness, difficulty with functional independence, or inadequate social support.

Social and Cultural Correlates of Mental Health and Illness

Although a number of social and cultural factors affect the mental health and development of elderly persons, gender, socioeconomic status, negative life events, physical health, race and ethnicity, and social support appear to be particularly strong influences (Dean, Kolody and Wood, 1990; Haug, Belgrave and Gratton, 1984; House et al., 1992).

Not only are these variables related to mental health, they are linked together in ways that profoundly influence the well-being of older adults. For example, depressed elderly persons are more likely to be women, unmarried or widowed, and of lower socioeconomic status, to have experienced stressful life events, to lack a supportive social network, and to have a coexisting physical condition (Blazer, Hughes and George, 1987; NIH Consensus Development Conference Statement, 1991). House and his colleagues have identified a differential exposure to psychosocial risk factors (health behaviors, social support, stress, and self-efficacy) across social strata. Further, they characterize the differential impact of these risk factors according to age groups as the "social stratification of aging and health."

Gender

The data about gender and elder mental health suggest that women are at somewhat greater risk for mental health problems, particularly depression and anxiety (Blazer, Hughes and George, 1987; Dean, Kolody and Wood, 1990; Holzer, Leaf and Weissman, 1985; Nacoste and Wise, 1991; Regier et al., 1988), whereas men are more likely to be diagnosed with substance use disorders or antisocial personality. For both men and women over age 65, rates of these disorders are lower than for younger adults.

In both the ECA studies and international data, the female-to-male prevalence of major depression was found to be almost 2 to 1 (Bebbington, 1990; Regier et al., 1988). Although the international data suggest that women are approximately twice as likely as men to develop mental disorders, these cross-cultural comparisons generally fail to account for substance use, antisocial personalities, and cognitive impairments, all of which are more prevalent in men (Bebbington, 1990; Regier et al., 1988). For older persons living in the United States, the female and male prevalence for all mental disorders is 13.6 percent and 10.5 percent, respectively.

Current depression was found to have a strong association with future depression (Phifer and Murrell, 1986); thus older women with severe depression probably experienced depressive episodes when younger. First-time depression in women after age 65 has been thought to be relatively infrequent, unless associated with bereavement (Holzer,

7

Leaf and Weissman, 1985). Loss, a significant and frequent occurrence among aged persons, is often accompanied by transient depressive symptoms. Women, who tend to live longer and are the majority of the oldest old, may be at greater risk for bereavement-related depression. Feinson (1987), however, in a comparison of community-dwelling bereaved and nonbereaved respondents, found that gender was correlated with general distress and depression only among the bereaved. Even so, when sociodemographic variables of race, age, marital status, education, and income were controlled, gender differences vanished.

Gender alone was not predictive of psychosomatic distress, emotional distress, or life satisfaction among rural elders (Revicki and Mitchell, 1990). Gender, as well as age and marital status, was not associated with changes in psychological symptoms over the course of a year, according to a study of elderly persons by Haug and associates (1984). Women, however, were more likely to report physical health problems. Given that somatic symptoms are often associated with depression, the tendency toward somatization may affect the assessment of depressive affect in women. Thus, data on national and international gender differences and similarities in mental health patterns indicate that diagnostic criteria and sociocultural factors may be connected to the perception of greater psychological impairment in older females.

Socioeconomic Status

Economic security is crucial to the mental health and well-being of older adults. Economic strain is associated with poor mental health (Moritz, Kasl and Berkman, 1989), lower life satisfaction (Chappell and Badger, 1989; Revicki and Mitchell, 1990), and depressive symptoms (Dean, Kolody and Wood, 1990; Krause, 1991). Economic factors may also underlie the apparent associations between gender and race and ethnicity with mental health because elderly women and minorities are more likely to hold lower socioeconomic positions. In a sample of 3,617 adults, for example, House and his colleagues (1992) found socioeconomic status to be related to morbidity, functional status, and limitations in daily activities—especially in later middle age and early old age. The prevalence of chronic health conditions among people 35–44 years of age in the lowest socioeconomic group was similar to the prevalence of chronic conditions of those 75 years and older in the highest socioeconomic stratum (House et al., 1992). Not surprisingly, older adults with lower education were found to have more financial problems and to be more depressed than those with higher education (Krause, 1991).

Issues of financial status may exert a powerful effect on the mental well-being of older persons of both sexes. In a study of the impact of living with a cognitively impaired spouse, for example, men who perceived their financial support as inadequate experienced more depressive symptoms (Moritz, Kasl and Berkman, 1989). Changes in financial security brought about by job loss, retirement, or other economic forces may jeopardize resources available to elders coping with a variety of stressors.

Negative Life Events

Negative life events, within changing social and cultural contexts, test the coping skills of older adults. Aging persons continue to experience a range of life events, which may adversely affect their mental health. Both recent and cumulative negative life events have been associated with poorer health outcomes, underscoring the impact of social and cultural status on health (House et al., 1992). Stressful life events, for example, were associated with decreases in self-esteem and mastery in a sample of elderly African Americans (Krause and Van Tran, 1989). Negative life events (Dean et al., 1990; Nacoste and Wise, 1991), particularly the death of a loved one (Blazer, Hughes and George, 1987; Feinson, 1987), have been associated with depression in the elderly. Despite conditions of overwhelming environmental press, older adults can be helped to integrate negative changes through supportive therapy.

Physical Health

Physical health is highly correlated with mental well-being in older adults. Illness, disability, and impairment in activities of daily living have been linked with lower life satisfaction and more psychological symptomatology (Blazer, Hughes and George, 1987; Chappell and Badger, 1989; Haug, Belgrave and Gratton, 1984; Revicki and Mitchell, 1990). Physical health and social support were found to be the strongest predictors of depression onset in a sample of adults over age 55 (Phifer and Murrell, 1986).

The extent to which physical and mental health problems are entwined is often unrecognized (Wykle and Kaskel, 1991). In a study of psychological dysfunction and the physical health of 150 elderly male inpatients (Rapp, Parisi and Walsh, 1988), 15 percent were found to have a diagnosis of either major, minor, or intermittent depression. Those diagnosed with depression had poorer physical health and greater psychological distress than their counterparts, yet none was diagnosed as being depressed. The ECA Program data on psychiatric diagnosis and medical service use (Kessler et al., 1987) indicate that roughly 22 percent of medical service users have a mental health diagnosis (anxiety, affective, or substance abuse disorder) and that approximately one-third of them talk with their care provider about the distress they experienced. By and large, however, these problems are unrecognized by providers.

Race and Ethnicity

The relationship between race and ethnicity and mental health is often affected by socioeconomic factors. Although the distinctions between the cultural effects of race and ethnicity on mental health and those connected with minority status are not always explicit, minority status seems to exert a separate effect (Markides and Mindel, 1987). For example, knowledge is lacking about the mental health effects of discrimination on aged cohorts who grew up in this country when bias was legal. Perceptions of mental health and tolerance of mental illness thus differ by race, ethnicity, and income (Faulkner, 1991). A limited but expanding data base about race, ethnicity, and elder mental health exists, particularly for blacks, Asian Americans, Native Americans, and Hispanics.

The data suggest that rates of depression and emotional distress among blacks are comparable to those of whites (Revicki and Mitchell, 1990; Stanford and DuBois, 1992). The ECA data indicate no differences between blacks and whites in a six-month prevalence study of major depression (Somervell et al., 1989). The data of Somervell and associates do suggest, however, that black men may have a tendency toward psychological distress that does not reach clinical proportions. Income, age, education, marital status, and social network contacts also may be associated with mental health among blacks (Jackson and Wolford, 1992; Stanford and DuBois, 1992).

While some studies have shown blacks to have higher life satisfaction than whites (Deimling, Harel and Noelker, 1983; Ortega, Crutchfield and Rushing, 1983), elderly rural blacks were found to have lower life satisfaction than rural whites (Revicki and Mitchell, 1990). Johnson and colleagues (1988) reported that whites had the highest life satisfaction, followed by blacks and American Indians, who had equivalent life satisfaction scores. Hispanics had the lowest life satisfaction and the poorest mental health when compared with the other groups (Johnson et al., 1988).

Elder Hispanics have high illiteracy and poverty rates (Sanchez, 1992), which tend to jeopardize their mental health. Depression is particularly prevalent among older Hispanic women, especially those who are widowed, have little education and low income, and are non–English speaking (Stanford and DuBois, 1992).

Native Americans have been identified as having high rates of depression and alcoholism. However, little research has been conducted on the mental health of Native American elders (Stanford and DuBois, 1992). Although the results of one study (Johnson et al., 1988) found life satisfaction among Native Americans to be adequate, their mental health scores spanned a wide range.

As with other minority groups, few studies address the problems of elderly Asian persons. Asian Americans, many of whom are recent immigrants, are dealing with language barriers, involuntary resettlement, and the stress of acculturation (Sakauye, 1992; Stanford and DuBois, 1992). Further, the stereotype of intergenerational family solidarity and closeness needs to be examined for its continuity in the American culture (Sakauye, 1992).

Meeting the mental health needs of minority elders poses unique challenges in that they are less likely to seek help. Moreover, they require mental health service providers who are culturally competent. Future epidemiologic research on within-culture and cross-cultural patterns requires recognition of "culture-bound syndromes," translation and norming of instruments for use with non-English-speaking clients, as well as the development of valid, reliable, and culturally sensitive measures (Sakauye, 1992).

Social Support

Social support is paramount to the mental health of older persons. Older adults who are part of a supportive social network are less likely to be depressed (Krause, 1991), especially when faced with illness or physical limitations. Phifer and Murrell (1986) found that over and above the direct effects that low support, poor physical health, and loss events had in relation to the onset of depression, those with low social support and poor health or a recent loss were at even greater risk for developing depressive symptomatology. Thus, higher levels of social support may offer protection to the mental health of older adults.

In examining the supportive dimensions of social networks, researchers have found that support is more than just an absolute count of social contacts (Chappell and Badger, 1989). Although more social contacts have been found to be associated with less emotional distress (Revicki and Mitchell, 1990), quantitative measures of contact with others, including one's spouse, may not be related to life satisfaction or global happiness (Chappel and Badger, 1989). The expressive and instrumental components of social support are especially relevant to the mental health and well-being of older adults. Elderly individuals who receive satisfactory instrumental support, such as assistance with household maintenance, appear to have less psychosomatic and emotional distress and greater life satisfaction (Revicki and Mitchell, 1990).

Affective support from spouses, friends, and confidants emerges as an important correlate of mental well-being. A high degree of expressive support from an elderly spouse has been associated with less depression, and low spousal support was found to have a greater effect on depressive symptoms than widowhood (Dean, Kolody and Wood, 1990). Those who live with others and have companion support were found to have the highest life satisfaction, whereas married elders who believed they had no companions were the least happy (Chappell and Badger, 1989). Similarly, Moritz and colleagues (1989) reported that cognitive impairment in wives was significantly associated with depressive symptomatology in the caregiver husbands, but the converse did not hold true. Perhaps the lack of a confidant, a role previously filled by the impaired wife, was related to the male caregiver's depression, whereas women are likely to have developed other social contacts over the years.

Friendships in later life may be as important as elders' relationships with adult children. Chappell and Badger (1989) found that being childless was not related to life satisfaction or well-being. Taylor and Chatters (1991) found that while adult children might foster the integration of black elders within the family network, elders' proximity to other relatives, but not immediate family, was related to satisfaction

12

with family life. The relationships between generations and those with friends are complex, and older persons may hold different expectations for each. Support from friends was found to have a stronger inverse relationship with depression than did support from children (Dean, Kolody and Wood, 1990), and perceived support from both family and church networks was correlated with well-being in elderly blacks (Walls and Zarit, 1991).

Religion is an important source of support and coping for elderly persons across many cultural groups, particularly for blacks. Involvement in organized religion was associated with greater self-esteem; nonorganized religiosity was associated with greater personal control in a sample of older blacks (Krause and Van Tran, 1989). Black caregivers of dementia patients were found to use religion first as a means of coping, whereas white caregivers tended to report using other strategies (Wykle and Segal, 1991).

There is a dearth of studies about ethnic and cultural differences in patterns and sources of social support. It is expected that variations within cultural groups would be as great as those between groups. While ethnic families of many cultures have been found to provide care to aging members, the choice of informal care rather than formal care may be related to socioeconomic factors, degree of acculturation, and social network structure (Antonucci and Cantor, 1991; Lockery, 1991).

PRACTICE IMPLICATIONS

While social and cultural factors play a significant role in the mental health of older persons, there is room for additional clarification of these relationships. There is some evidence that social support and confidants are central to the mental well-being of elderly people, but more knowledge in this area needs to be developed. Data suggest that socioeconomic factors, as well as race, ethnicity, and gender affect the mental health of elders. Interestingly, gender seems to be associated with depression across cultures, casting doubt on gender differences related solely to socioeconomic status, but perhaps underscoring the minority status of women.

Practitioners who provide general healthcare to aged individuals are in a good position to identify and refer those who need mental health treatment. While treatment for mental disorders in elderly persons may not yield complete remission of symptoms in all cases, distress and anxiety can be reduced enough to improve the quality of life. More important, efforts that promote mental and physical health across the life span may be crucial if we are to reduce certain types of physical and cognitive impairment related to social and cultural factors. Increasing the numbers of culturally competent and sensitive therapists and practitioners who provide service to aged persons is a priority, especially as the social definitions of minority status change.

References

Antonucci, T. and Cantor, M., 1991. "Strengthening the Family Support System for Older Minority Persons." In *Minority Elders: Longevity, Economics and Health.* Washington, DC: Gerontological Society of America.

Baltese, P., Reese, H. and Lipsitt, L., 1980. "Life-Span Developmental Psychology." *Annual Review of Psychology* 31: 65–110.

Bebbington, P., 1990. "Population Surveys of Psychiatric Disorder and the Need for Treatment." *Social Psychiatry and Psychiatric Medicine* 25: 33–40.

Blazer, D., Hughes, D. and George, L., 1987. "The Epidemiology of Depression in an Elderly Community Population." *Gerontologist* 27(3): 281–87.

Burns, B. and Taub, C., 1990. "Mental Health Services in General Medical Care and in Nursing Homes." In B. Fogel, A. Furino and G. Gottlieb, eds., *Mental Health Policy for Older Americans: Protecting Minds at Risk.* Washington, DC: American Psychiatric Press, pp. 63–83.

Chappell N. and Badger, M., 1989. "Social Isolation and Well-Being." *Journal of Gerontology* 44(5): S169–76.

Dean, A., Kolody, B. and Wood, P., 1990. "Effects of Social Support from Various Sources on Depression in Elderly Persons." *Journal of Health and Social Behavior* 31: 148–61.

Deimling, G., Harel, Z. and Noelker, L., 1983. "Racial Differences in Social Integration and Life Satisfaction Among Aged Public Housing Residents." *International Journal of Aging and Human Development* 17: 203–12.

Faulkner, A., 1991. "Culture, Chronic Mental Illness, and the Aged: Research Issues and Directions." In E. Light and B. Lebowitz, eds., *The*

Elderly with Chronic Mental Illness. New York: Springer Publishing Co.

Feinson, M., 1987. "Mental Health and Aging: Are There Gender Differences?" *Gerontologist* 27(6): 703–11.

Gatz, M. and Smyer, M., 1992. "The Mental Health System and Older Adults in the 1990's." *American Psychologist* 47(6): 741–51.

Haug, M., Belgrave, L. and Gratton, B., 1984. "Mental Health and the Elderly: Factors in Stability and Change Over Time." *Journal of Health and Social Behavior* 25: 100–115.

Holzer, C., Leaf, P. and Weissman, M., 1985. "Living With Depression." In M. Haug, A. Ford and M. Schaefor, eds., *The Physical and Mental Health of Aged Women.* New York: Springer Publishing Co., pp. 101–16.

House, J. et al., 1992. "Social Stratification, Age, and Health." In K. W. Schaie, D. Blazer and J. House, eds., *Aging, Health Behaviors, and Health Outcomes.* Hillsdale, NJ: Lawrence Erlbaum Associates, pp. 1–32.

Jackson, J. and Wolford, M., 1992. "Changes from 1980 to 1987 in Mental Health Status and Help-Seeking Among African Americans." *Journal of Geriatric Psychiatry* 25(1): 15–67.

Johnson, F. et al., 1988. "Comparison of Mental Health and Life Satisfaction of Five Elderly Ethnic Groups." *Western Journal of Nursing Research* 10(5): 613–28.

Kessler, L. et al., 1987. "Psychiatric Diagnoses of Medical Service Users: Evidence from the Epidemiologic Catchment Area Program." *American Journal of Public Health* 77(1): 18–24.

Koenig, H. and Blazer, D., 1992. "Mood Disorders and Suicide." In J. E. Birren, R. B. Sloan and G. Cohen, eds., *Handbook of Mental Health and Aging.* San Diego, CA: Academic Press, pp. 379–407.

Krause, N., 1991. "Stress and Isolation from Close Ties in Later Life." *Journal of Gerontology* 46(4): S183–94.

Krause, N. and Van Tran, T., 1989. "Stress and Religious Involvement Among Older Blacks." *Journal of Gerontology* 44(1): S4–13.

Lockery, S., 1991. "Family and Social Supports: Caregiving Among Racial and Ethnic Minority Elders." *Generations* 15(4): 58–62.

Markides, K. and Mindel, C., 1987. *Aging and Ethnicity.* Newbury Park, CA: Sage.

Moritz, D., Kasl, S. and Berkman, L., 1989. "The Health Impact of Living with a Cognitively Impaired Spouse: Depressive Symptoms and Social

Functioning." *Journal of Gerontology* 44(1): S17–27.

Nacoste, D. and Wise, W., 1991. "The Relationship Among Negative Life Events, Cognitions, and Depression Within Three Generations." *Gerontologist* 31(3): 397–403.

Nagley, S. et al., 1988. "Age Cohort Comparison in an Acute Psychiatric Setting." *Gerontologist* 28: 39A.

National Institutes of Health, 1991. "Diagnosis and Treatment of Depression in Late Life." (Reprinted from NIH Consensus Development Conference Consensus Statement, 1991, Nov. 4–6. Washington, DC)

Ortega, S., Crutchfield, R. and Rushing, W., 1983. "Race Differences in Elderly Personal Well-Being." *Research on Aging* 5: 101–18.

Phifer, J. and Murrell, S., 1986. "Etiologic Factors in the Onset of Depressive Symptoms in Older Adults." *Journal of Abnormal Psychology* 95(3): 282–91.

Rabins, P., 1992. "Prevention of Mental Disorder in the Elderly: Current Perspectives and Future Prospects." *Journal of the American Geriatrics Society* 40(7): 727–33.

Rapp, S., Parisi, S. and Walsh, D., 1988. "Psychological Dysfunction and Physical Health Among Elderly Medical Inpatients." *Journal of Consulting and Clinical Psychology* 56(6): 851–55.

Regier, D. et al., 1988. "One-Month Prevalence of Mental Disorders in the United States." *Archives of General Psychiatry* 45: 977–86.

Revicki, D. and Mitchell, J., 1990. "Strain, Social Support, and Mental Health in Rural Elderly Individuals." *Journal of Gerontology* 45(6): S267–74.

Rubenstein, R. et al., 1991. "Key Relationships of Never Married, Childless Older Women: A Cultural Analysis." *Journal of Gerontology* 46(5): S270–77.

Sakauye, K., 1992. "The Elderly Asian Patient." *Journal of Geriatric Psychiatry* 25(1): 85–105.

Sanchez, C., 1992. "Mental Health Issues: The Elderly Hispanic." *Journal of Geriatric Psychiatry* 25(1): 69–84.

Somervell, P. et al., 1989. "The Prevalence of Major Depression in Black and White Adults in Five United States Communities." *American Journal of Epidemiology* 130(4): 725–35.

Stanford, E. P. and DuBois, B., 1992. "Gender and Ethnicity Patterns." In J. E. Birren, R. B. Sloan and G. Cohen, eds., *Handbook of Mental Health and Aging.* San Diego, CA: Academic Press, pp. 99–115.

Taylor, R. and Chatters, L., 1991. "Extended Family Networks of Older Blacks." *Journal of Gerontology* 46(4): S210–17.

Walls, C. and Zarit, S., 1991. "Informal Support from Black Churches and Well-Being of Elderly Blacks." *Gerontologist* 31(4): 490–95.

Wykle, M. and Kaskel, B., 1991. "Increasing the Longevity of Minority Older Adults Through Improved Health Status." In *Minority Elders: Longevity, Economics and Health.* Washington, DC: Gerontological Society of America, pp. 24–31.

Wykle, M. and Segal, M., 1991. "A Comparison of Black and White Family Caregivers' Experience with Dementia." *Journal of the Black Nurses Association* 5(1): 29–41.

Wykle, M. and Musil, C., in press. "Developmental Issues in Gerontology." *Proceedings of the State of the Science Congress on Nursing Research and its Utilization.* Washington, DC

Wykle, M., Segal, M. and Nagley, S., 1992. "Mental Health and Aging: Hospital Care—A Nursing Perspective." In J. E. Birren, R. B. Sloan and G. Cohen, eds., *Handbook of Mental Health and Aging.* San Diego, CA: Academic Press, pp. 815–31.

Everyday Mental Health

A Guide to Assessing Life Strengths

Helen Q. Kivnick

nstead of thinking about old age primarily in terms of compensating for deficits, we must learn, as Finkel and Cohen (1982) recommended over 10 years ago, to think also in terms of maximizing human resources. And we must broaden our notion of elders' resources to include the vitality, the grit, the underlying commitment to values that constitute the infinite resources of the human spirit. Throughout life, this spirit sparkles in the people and relationships that inspire us to keep trying. It is what permits a pair of professional, middle-aged women to care for their 85-year-old mother-in-law—suddenly blind and reluctantly transplanted from the rural South to the urban North—and to have all of them draw strength from the process. It is what permits the 92-year-old granddaughter of a slave to remain active in her church and maintain a long-held clerical position despite nearly crippling arthritis. We must understand the dynamics of this spirit, nurture it, and learn to use it to fullest advantage. And instead of thinking of mental health in old age either as an absence of identifiable disorders or in terms of decontextualized measures of life satisfaction, we must learn to view it in terms of this vitality of spirit.

Life-cycle scholars argue for the continuity of developmental psychosocial processes throughout the entire life cycle (Erikson, 1950; Levinson et al., 1978; Taylor and Ford, 1981; Erikson, Erikson and

Kivnick, 1986; Kaufman, 1986; Thompson, 1992). Considering our aging population in terms of life-cycle theory suggests that we move beyond concern for compensating and remediating toward the following: (1) working with elders by building on past strengths; (2) encouraging the middle-aged and the young-old to prepare for old age by thoughtful anticipation; and (3) promoting intergenerational interaction for the psychosocial benefit of both the old and the not-yet-old.

The most recent formulations of Erikson's life-cycle developmental theory (Erikson, Erikson and Kivnick, 1986; Kivnick, in press) describe eight psychosocial themes as a kind of scaffolding around which people construct their lives, from beginning to end (see Figure 2.1).

Fundamental to the uniqueness of each individual's life and psychosocial profile is the notion, illustrated in *Vital Involvement in Old Age* (Erikson, Erikson and Kivnick, 1986), that each theme—each pair of opposing tendencies—is enacted through characteristic behaviors and attitudes. Reciprocally, life's activities, experiences, feelings, and attitudes are all understood as somehow involved with balancing one theme or more. The essence of each theme is thought to be universal. That is, each theme exists as a central life motif, to be balanced by individuals in diverse cultures and subcultures throughout the world. However, from one culture to another we see tremendous variation in both thematic behavioral expressions and also in the nature of healthy, appropriate thematic balances. For example, hard work, learning, perseverance, self-discipline, mastery, and employment are central behavioral expressions of the theme of industry and inferiority in mainstream America in the late twentieth century. Behavioral and attitudinal expressions of this same theme may be quite different in different cultural settings.

In *Vital Involvement,* a section called "The Voices of Our Informants" considers the reflections, experiences, and philosophical musings of 29 aged Northern Californians in terms of each of the eight themes, in turn. Within common experiences of loss, debilitation, and constriction, these 29 elders differed widely in the vitality and resilience they brought to the process of living in old age. And these differences had everything to do with their individual psychosocial profiles, their life-long patterns of thematic strength and weakness. In this chapter, illustrations are drawn both from the 29 Northern California elders and also from respondents in subsequent research conducted in Chicago

	57	58	59	60	61	62	63	64
Older Adulthood	57	58	59	60	61	62	63	64 Integrity & Despair. WISDOM
Middle Adulthood	49	50	51	52	53	54	55 Generativity & Self-Absorption. CARE	56
Young Adulthood	41	42	43	44	45	46 Intimacy & Isolation. LOVE	47	48
Adolescence	33	34	35	36	37 Identity & Confusion. FIDELITY	38	39	40
School Age	25	26	27	28 Industry & Inferiority. COMPETENCE	29	30	31	32
Play Age	17	18	19 Initiative & Guilt. PURPOSE	20	21	22	23	24
Toddler-hood	9	10 Autonomy & Shame/Doubt. WILL	11	12	13	14	15	16
Infancy	1 Basic Trust & Basic Mistrust. HOPE	2	3	4	5	6	7	8

FIGURE 2.1 Psychosocial Themes and Stages of Life

NOTE: Box numbers do not correspond to particular ages or years. Rather, they provide a convenient way to refer to specific boxes.

SOURCE: Adapted from Erikson, E. H., Erikson, J. M. and Kivnick, H. Q., *Vital Involvement in Old Age* (New York: W. W. Norton & Co., 1986). Used with permission of the publisher.

and in Minnesota's Twin Cities. Throughout the life cycle and for all themes, three principles are central to Erikson's reformulated theory: dynamic balance of opposites, anticipating and renewing, and vital involvement.

DYNAMIC BALANCE OF OPPOSITES

For each psychosocial theme, individuals are involved in balancing personal strengths and weaknesses—skills and clumsinesses, capacities and deficits, interests and ignorances—in an ongoing attempt to live satisfying lives in a world of people, places, materials, institutions, ideas, organizations, and more. Dystonic tendencies are brought into dynamic balance with syntonic, each catalyzing the other and relying on the other for its own meaning. School age's inevitable inferiorities, for example, induce increased efforts at industriousness and mastery. Without industry's rewards, feelings of inferiority can overwhelm and paralyze; without inferiority's goading reminders, feelings of capability can inflate to lose all grounding in reality.

ANTICIPATING AND RENEWING

Overall epigenetic psychosocial development, i.e., the lifelong process of balancing psychosocial themes, is thought to be a product both of biology and of the environment. Like cognition and physical stature, psychosocial capacities develop according to a genetic program, under the influence of a great number of environmental factors. The specific time of each theme's ascendancy is determined by an interaction between biological possibility and the age-grade system that determines each culture's marking of social time (Neugarten and Datan, 1973).

Each theme comes to ascendancy at one stage or another (as toddlers, for example, focus enormous amounts of energy on balancing a sense of willfulness and independence with ever-present, necessary feelings of doubt). But all themes are operational at every stage in the life cycle, and psychosocial development takes place in all 64 boxes of the life-cycle chart. Themes that will be focal in adulthood are previewed or anticipated in early life, as, for example, a Play Aged child "preworks" Generativity and Self-Absorption through playing house, caring for pets, and helping caretakers comfort younger siblings (see Figure 2.1, box 23). Themes that are focal in childhood are revisited and reviewed in subsequent stages. Even those themes that are adequately balanced when ascendant must perpetually be reworked in terms that are newly age-appropriate. For example, the Toddler's struggle to balance Autonomy with Shame/Doubt focuses on specific issues that include toilet training, walking and talking, early self-esteem, and obedience to authority (see Figure 2.1, box 10). In Older Adulthood this same theme resurfaces around issues of self-reliance and dependency, of stubbornness and compliance, of control and helplessness (see Figure 2.1, box 58). Satisfactory earlier-life balancing of this pair of opposing tendencies and lifelong experiences of meeting thematic challenges with appropriate behaviors and attitudes all maximize the likelihood of effective later-life renewing.

By old age this process of lifelong balancing has led, ideally, to the development of thematic strengths that are robust and resilient, that rest on myriad different experiences and continue to draw on them all. The need to continue to work at "early" themes in later life is a function of current life demands and is not a direct product of thematic success or failure. Clearly, then, the notion of old age as a time to sit back and reap the psychosocial fruits of earlier efforts must yield to a more realistic view of ongoing, always dynamic reinvolvement, reviewing, renewing, and reworking.

VITAL INVOLVEMENT

At each stage throughout the life cycle, themes are balanced or "worked on" as they are enacted through involvement in everyday feelings, activities, dreams, relationships, and more. It is this vital involvement that gives psychosocial process—a synthesis of the psychological and internal with the social and external—its full meaning.

This vigorous psychosocial process provides a useful way to conceptualize everyday mental health: not as an entity to be acquired, but as a process to be engaged; not as a state to be attained apart from life's vicissitudes, but as a means of living life itself; not only in childhood and youth, but in middle and older adulthood as well. It is not an actuality to be assessed at one moment, apart from past and future. Mental health at any age is part and parcel of the epigenetic development that drives the life course from beginning to end. And mental health is inextricably intertwined with the inner and outer experiences that compose that life course.

Baltes (1991) and Baltes and Baltes (1990) discuss a strategy for old-age mastery and adaptation based on a model of optimization through selection and compensation. Although their model is presented primarily in terms of observable behaviors, its mechanisms are compatible with the notion presented here of later-life mental health as psychosocial process that maximizes thematic strengths. Throughout the life cycle, everyday mental health may be described as an attempt to live meaningfully, in a particular set of social and environmental circumstances, relying on a particular collection of resources and supports. Simply said, we all try to do the best we can with what we have. Part of this effort involves developing internal strengths and capacities; part involves identifying and using external resources; part involves compensating for weaknesses and deficits. The whole process may be understood as thematic vital involvement with the people, places, materials, living things, institutions, and ideas that make up the world in which we all live. For each theme, old age presents new challenges to existing capacity and poses special opportunities for new growth. As in earlier life, elders work to meet these thematic challenges by drawing on a unique set of personal balances between thematic strengths and weaknesses, based on the efforts and products of a lifetime.

As physical strengths diminish and external supports fade away, internal strength and health become increasingly important to every elder's ongoing integrity. Compensatory services may be necessary for maintaining day-to-day survival, but day-to-day survival is the starting—and not the ending—point of life, at every stage. In addition to meeting functional needs, elder services should be designed to promote the unique patterns of individual involvement and life strength that constitute everyday mental health. To be sure, it may be a straightforward matter to try and arrange for every older woman to receive those services that offset a standard list of functional deficits. How much more respectful it is to arrange for those services that will allow each unique older woman to be as strong, as competent, as resilient, as much herself as possible.

With appropriate encouragement, a passive, apathetic older man can become involved, once again, with the ideas, activities, and people that once gave his life meaning. When he becomes an active part of a telephone support network, he is providing for his peers a checkup service that need not be supplied by outsiders. When he participates in a group that writes letters for Amnesty International or that lobbies on behalf of legalizing living wills, other group members may find themselves helping him pick up groceries as an easy extension of their collegiality. When he tells the jokes that have always made people laugh, he asserts an element of his lifelong identity. Moreover, he may make it possible for service providers and case manager alike to leave him feeling enlivened and rejuvenated rather than depleted from serving just one more incapacitated client. Appropriate planning and encouragement can help this older man become an active participant in a life characterized by vitality. In so doing, he begins to give something back at a time when he is probably accepting far more than his adult sensibilities tolerate with comfort. This kind of vital involvement in life is precisely what gives rise to psychosocial health and strength—to everyday mental health—at any age.

Central to promoting everyday mental health in the aging is identifying and attending to their life strengths. What are the particular activities, interests, relationships, and values that have characterized a given elder throughout life? Has one man always taken pride in being a dapper dresser? Has another deliberately purchased goods and services in such a way as to express support for organized labor? Does a third rely on reading the morning paper, front to back, for his sense of grounding in the world?

Underlying these specific behavioral expressions, what are the psychosocial themes on which each elder has relied in meeting life's ordinary expectations and in coping with extraordinary challenges? Does a woman acclimate herself to new surroundings by seeking companionship? Or does she put most of her energy into setting up her new household and meticulously arranging her belongings? Or does she look for a job—paid or volunteer—that will let her continue to exercise her accounting skills? When she needs comfort, does she call a friend? Or say a prayer? Or fix herself a delicious pot of spaghetti? When she is in a tight spot, does she ask for help? Or insist on self-reliance? Does she work hard at implementing solutions that have succeeded in the past? Or does she devise a new course of action that seems uniquely suited to this current situation?

How does any given elder express his or her unique balance around each theme? Does a man make confident decisions only after discussion with trusted friends? Or does he keep his own counsel, regarding outside advice as intruding on his autonomy? Or does he rely on one particular advisor to make a suggestion that he then experiences as his own? What are the themes around which each elder has difficulty? Perhaps a man has always been able to make appropriate decisions, but has never been good at following through. Perhaps he has always worked hard and well at implementing ideas that originated with someone else. Perhaps he has never been someone even his closest friends could count on in a pinch.

Understanding each elder's unique profile of thematic life strengths and weaknesses allows for the planning of later life in such a way as to maximize everyday mental health—to exercise existing strengths, to develop new strengths, and to use personal strengths to balance out personal weaknesses and environmental deficits. Regardless of age or stage, we all deserve to be as alive as we can be, to exchange—to receive and to contribute—as much as we can with the outside world, to derive as much satisfaction as possible from each day of living. Identifying meaningful activities and interests would seem to be a straightforward process. Building these activities and interests into daily life would seem to be so logical as to be taken for granted. But even these first steps are often overlooked for the frail elderly, as case managers, family members, and elders themselves rush to organize care plans. It is certainly understandable, then, that we find ourselves all but ignoring the thematic strengths and weaknesses that underlie specific behaviors. (See chapter 9 for suggestions on how to build these considerations into assessment approaches.)

Thematic patterns of strengths and weakness and the specific behaviors through which individuals enact these patterns are the very essence of the mental health that leads one wheelchair-bound, arthritic granny to make the traditional Christmas tamales with her children each year, while another bemoans her miserable life, demands attention and service, and criticizes the efforts of all those who try to provide. Long-term care has been identified as the national crisis of the coming decades. Attending to life strengths can help us respond to this crisis and, simultaneously, promote the psychosocial health that is an infinite resource available to us all.

How do we attend to life strengths? How do we assess them, identify them, and use them in a practical way? The *Life Strengths Interview Guide* that follows is being developed to help case managers, family members, and elder clients come to know the thematic life strengths and values that constitute the core of each elder's unique sense of self in the world (Kivnick, 1991). Understanding this core is essential to developing a life plan; that is, a plan of activities and services, formal and informal, behavioral and emotional, to maximize elder vitality and contribution, along with meeting functional needs. The guide is based on empirical and theoretical knowledge of the specific behaviors and attitudes that most often express each theme (Erikson, Erikson and Kivnick, 1986); its questions are designed to elicit information about life strengths associated with all eight themes. This information can then suggest very specific strategies for maximizing a given elder's strengths and for helping this same elder begin to rework thematic weaknesses.

The interview guide can serve two additional important functions. First, it can help elders begin to think, quite specifically, about issues that many of us either take for granted or never quite take the time to clarify for ourselves at all. This kind of self-reflection is a central psychosocial task of the final stage in the life cycle (Birren and Deutchman, 1991; Butler, 1963; Erikson, 1950; Erikson, Erikson and Kivnick, 1986; see also chapter 8). Second, discussing these issues out loud can help forge meaningful bonds between the people involved. For case managers and clients who will be working together for a long time to come, these bonds can promote the mutuality that enriches all relationships. For family caregivers and elder relatives, such bonds can reintroduce elements of personality, shared history, and respect into relationships that are too often dominated by senses of duty and guilt, by daily tasks, and by attitudes and exchanges that were routinized decades before. In a context of long-term care, the interview guide is designed to be used in conjunction with traditional assessment instruments.

Many elders value the opportunity to explore the kinds of issues raised in this interview. Especially after dwelling on their difficulties in bathing and dressing themselves, for example, they are eager to talk about what it is that gives them a sense of hope and security. For those who seem to regard some of the interview questions as vague, meaningless, or intrusive, an explanation like the one that follows often helps put them at ease. "You've talked a lot about the things you have trouble with these days. But there's more to you than your problems. If we talk about the things you do well and enjoy, we can try to plan a program that will help you continue to be as strong as possible. And if I can get an idea about your underlying philosophy of life, about what things really matter most to you, it will help me take those things into account in our work together."

This interview guide is designed to open up aspects of elders' lives that remain, far too often, closed off from case managers, family members, and personal awareness, as well. Once these aspects are open, the guide helps us understand them in terms of an individual's overall psychosocial profile, and use them in promoting the everyday mental health that underlies overall well-being. The guide is not a checklist. It does not yield a simple, numerical score that corresponds to a specific course of action. Rather, it organizes a large amount of information into eight overall life themes. Once the issues have all been discussed, it is up to case managers, family caregivers, and elders to interpret this wealth of data and translate it into a unique profile of life strengths. This profile holds the key to planning that reflects concern for the elder's *life* as well as for his or her *care*. It allows us to help each elder live out the last years of life by playing to his or her strengths.

Although some elders and interviewers may enjoy conducting the interview in one or two long, concentrated sessions, most will probably prefer discussing this material over the course of several meetings. And for many, these are issues to be reconsidered and rediscussed, in different ways, over time. As noted earlier, life strengths are not static or fixed, to be evaluated once and then used as a standard forevermore. Like life itself, life strengths shift and sway as part of an overall picture that is always changing. And particularly when we seek to make strengths conscious and then to invigorate them further, ongoing consideration is an integral part of the process.

The guide is presented in its detailed entirety as an answer to two often-asked questions: (1) How can I get my aging client/relative to start talking about any of these issues? (2) Where is any of this published so that I can look at it, think about it, and begin to use it in my own work/life? Questions are arranged thematically. Within each theme, questions need not be asked in the order or precise words in which they appear; specific questions need not be asked at all. Probes and explanations in italics are intended as asides, written to interviewers to assist them in conducting discussions that are as complete as possible. This material may be used as examples, if elders have trouble answering questions, or it may be paraphrased or replaced with other examples at the interviewer's discretion. The guide is intended to assist and to illustrate, not to be comprehensive or to be administered verbatim.

One question may trigger many associations in the elder's mind, and these associations may answer questions that have not yet been asked. The questions are simply tools to encourage elders to think and talk seriously about who they are, what matters to them, and what they think about the issues that matter most. Far more important than the answer to any specific question is the overall pattern of life stories, values, and strengths that we hope each elder will bring to light. The guide is designed to facilitate both this discovery and the subsequent processes of thematic understanding, interpretation, and integration into life planning. Rather than worrying about getting specific questions or probes just right, interviewers must be familiar with the entire guide. They should understand the notions of thematic life strengths, behavioral expressions, and everyday mental health. Everything else will follow.

LIFE STRENGTHS INTERVIEW GUIDE

INTRODUCTION

What is it about your life:

…that is most worth living for?

…that makes you feel most alive?

…that makes you feel most like yourself?

[Probe: These can be things that may seem quite small, like brewing Earl Gray tea in your familiar china teapot, or working at your computer, or cooking the dishes you've been making for decades. Or they may be things that seem larger, like making sure your grandchildren learn good values, or writing letters for Amnesty International, or voting, or working for causes you believe in.]

MENTAL HEALTH AND AGING

HOPE & FAITH (TRUST & MISTRUST)

What is it in your life that gives you hope?

How do moral beliefs and values fit into your life?

How have they fit in earlier times?

What is your religious affiliation?

What about religion is most important to you?

How do you like to express your religious beliefs?

Is religion something you practice in private? Is some group religious activity important to you?

What is it in your life that gives you a sense of security?

What do you tell yourself or think about when you're afraid and you need to believe that things will be all right?

WILLFULNESS, INDEPENDENCE, & CONTROL (AUTONOMY & SHAME/DOUBT)

(We all like to be in control of ourselves and our lives. And when you think about it, we spend most of our lives trying to strike a tolerable balance between being independent and having things the way we want them, on one hand, and accepting help and going along with other people's wishes, on the other hand.)

How is your health these days?

Do you:

…have any physical limitations?

…have any diseases or conditions for which you're being treated?

…take medications?

…rely on aids such as glasses, hearing aid, cane/walker/wheelchair, etc.?

…rely on assistance with homemaking, personal care, etc.?

What parts of your life is it most important that *you* stay in charge of?

What kinds of control are easier to give up, as long as you remain in charge of what's really important?

[Probe to prioritize autonomy-related issues in daily life. Levels of probe vary, depending on whether elder currently lives independently or in some kind of protected environment.

E.g.: What you eat; where you eat; when you eat; making your own food; feeding yourself; what you wear; dressing yourself; walking, toileting, and bathing yourself; who assists you with ADLs?

Daily routine:
> *Listen to radio and TV as you wish*
> *Use the telephone when you wish*
> *Go out and come back when you wish*
> *Have access to preferred reading materials*
> *Get-up time; mealtime; nap time; bedtime*

Living in your own home:
> *Decorate as you wish*
> *Save belongings as you wish*
> *Lock your door to keep out whomever you want to keep out*
> *Leave your house to whomever you choose*

Medical treatment:
> *Following doctor's orders as you wish*
> *Hospitalization vs. outpatient treatment*
> *Surgery vs. noninvasive treatment*
> *Respirators; artificial nutrition; artificial hydration*

Spending money:
> *Spend money on your own enjoyment*
> *Spend money on your own care*
> *Save money for a rainy day (What is a rainy day?)*
> *Save money to leave it to your heirs]*

What kinds of independence would you find especially painful to give up?

What do you think might make it easier to accept help, when you wish you didn't need help in the first place?

What is it that has always given you confidence in yourself?

What kinds of decisions are absolutely most important that you make for yourself?

What kinds of decisions are you willing to have someone else make for you? Who?

PURPOSEFULNESS, PLEASURE, & IMAGINATION (INITIATIVE & GUILT)

What kinds of things do you enjoy doing? What kinds of activities give you pleasure?

What kinds of activities have always given you pleasure?

[Probes: Eating; movies; walking; cooking; concerts; museums; library; parks; shopping; visiting with friends; travel; reading; writing; helping; babysitting;

radio; music; work with hands; care for plants; charity; volunteer work; church work; arts; sports; housecleaning; making things for people]

What do you do for fun these days?

What would you do for fun if you could do anything in the world?

What have you done, in your life, that makes you proudest?

What is there that you've always been curious about?

What do you want to do, most of all, with the rest of your life?

COMPETENCE & HARD WORK (INDUSTRY & INFERIORITY)

What have you worked hard at?

What would you like to be working at now, if you were able?

What kinds of things have you always been good at?

What kinds of things are you good at now? What skills do you have? Or areas of expertise?

[Probe: These may be professionally related skills like accounting or photography, or they may be personal skills like reading poetry, or cooking certain special dishes, or making phone calls.]

What is there that you've always wanted to learn, but never quite gotten around to?

What do you wish you could do better?

Would you find it easier to accept assistance if you could trade some skill or activity in return?

VALUES & SENSE OF SELF (IDENTITY & CONFUSION)

What is it about life that makes you feel most like yourself? Why do you think this activity or belief or relationship makes you feel this way?

What do you believe in?

Do you have a philosophy of life that has guided the way you live your life? That guides your life today?

What kind of person would you say:

…you are?

…you have always been?

What is the image that you carry around inside, about who you are in the world?

When people describe you, what do they say? What would you like them to say?

LOVE & FRIENDSHIP (*INTIMACY & ISOLATION*)

Who is important to you in your life today? Where do they live?

Whom do you count on these days? Who counts on you?

Whom do you have contact with these days?

Who, among these, are people you contact by choice?

Tell me about someone you've loved at some point in your life.

Can you tell me about:

...your marriage?

...your best friend?

What do the people who know you best like most about you? What do they respect most in you?

Who, in which relationships, has brought out the best in you?

How do you feel about being alone these days?

CARE & PRODUCTIVITY (*GENERATIVITY & SELF-ABSORPTION*)

Whom or what do you especially care about?

[Probe: What people, pets, ideas, activities, organizations and issues concern you? What plants and objects, people and issues are you sure to take care of?]

How do you show your caring?

Who is there that you lean on, these days? Who leans on you?

Who is there, that it's important to you to be good for? Or to be nice to? Or to set a good example for?

What is there about yourself and your life that you want to make sure people remember?

Who and what have you cared about over the years? Whom have you cared for? Taken care of? Tell me about them.

What's the most important thing for you to do with your life these days?

Who is the person who makes you think, "This is the one who will carry on for me when I'm gone"?

WISDOM & PERSPECTIVE (*INTEGRITY & DESPAIR*)

What is there about your life that you wish had been different?

What is there that you're struggling to make sense of, about the world?

What has been most meaningful about your life so far?

How do you deal with disappointment? How do you experience joy?
What strategies have you used for coping with fear?
Let's talk a bit about death:
What are your thoughts about:
…your own death?
…how you'd like to die?
…where you'd like to die?
…who should be there with you?
…anything you'd want to be sure and get done first?
…anything you'd want to be sure to say to anyone first?
…who should take what kinds of measures to prolong your life?
Have these thoughts changed over the years?
Are you afraid of dying?
Do you know what you're afraid of?
Do you have any ideas about what might help you be less afraid?

PUTTING IT ALL TOGETHER AGAIN

What is it about your life today that:
…makes you feel most alive?
…is most worth living for?
…makes you feel most like yourself?

I'd like you to think back over your whole life. Over everything you've seen and everything that's happened to you. And I'd like you to tell me a story about something in your life. Anything. But a story from your life that is somehow meaningful for you.

CONCLUSION

The last quarter of the twentieth century has seen a skyrocketing in the size of the oldest sector of our population. The fragility of these "oldest old" has made eldercare a major issue for planners, policy makers, practitioners, and family members throughout our society. Thus, interest in the health of the aging has taken a back seat to concern with illness, both physical and mental. Interest in well-being has been all but eclipsed by concern with the daily survival that often requires care and services to compensate for deficits and disabilities. Attention to everyday mental health in the aging can serve as a first step toward restoring appropriate balance both to individual lives and also to larger-scale programs and policies. It can help reequilibrate and revitalize both the lives of individual elders and the varied relationships that exist between people who are old and frail and those who are younger and hardier. In addition, consideration of everyday mental health in terms of life-long psychosocial themes can promote thoughtful anticipation of later life among those who are still young-old, middle aged, or younger. These processes are essential to weaving a fabric of life that is strong and resilient enough to sustain us, in all our humanity, from birth to death and from generation to generation. We must settle for no less.

References

Baltes, P. B., 1991. "The Many Faces of Human Ageing: Toward a Psychological Culture of Old Age." *Psychological Medicine* 21: 837–54.

Baltes P. B. and Baltes, M. M., 1990. "Psychological Perspectives on Successful Aging: The Model of Selective Optimization with Compensation." In P. B. Baltes and M. M. Baltes, eds., *Successful Aging: Perspectives from the Behavioral Sciences.* New York: Cambridge University Press, pp. 1–34.

Birren, J. E. and Deutchman, D. E., 1991. *Guiding Autobiography Groups for Older Adults: Exploring the Fabric of Life.* Baltimore, MD: The Johns Hopkins University Press.

Butler, R., 1963. "The Life Review: An Interpretation of Reminiscence in the Aged." *Psychiatry* 26: 65–76.

Erikson, E. H., 1950. *Childhood and Society.* New York: W. W. Norton.

Erikson, E. H., Erikson, J. M. and Kivnick, H. Q., 1986. *Vital Involvement in Old Age.* New York: W. W. Norton.

Finkel, S. I. and Cohen, G., 1982. "The Mental Health of the Aging." *Gerontologist* 22: 227–28.

Kaufman, S. R., 1986. *The Ageless Self.* New York: New American Library.

Kivnick, H. Q., 1991. *Living with Care; Caring for Life: The Inventory of Life Strengths.* (Available from the Long-Term Care Decisions Resource Center, School of Public Health, University of Minnesota, Minneapolis, MN 55455.)

Kivnick, H. Q., in press, "Through the Life Cycle: Psychosocial Thoughts on Old Age." In G. H. Pollock and S. I. Greenspan, eds., *The Course of Life*, vol. 5. Madison, CT: International Universities Press.

Levinson, D. L. et al., 1978. *The Seasons of a Man's Life*. New York: Ballantine Books.

Neugarten, B. L. and Datan, N., 1973. "Sociological Perspectives on the Life Cycle." In P. B. Baltes and K. W. Schaie, eds., *Life-Span Developmental Psychology: Personality and Socialization*. New York: Academic Press, pp. 53–69.

Taylor, R. and Ford, G., 1981. "Lifestyle and Ageing." *Ageing and Society* 1: 329–45.

Thompson, P., 1992. "I don't Feel Old." *Ageing and Society* 12: 23–48.

Family Network Perspectives on Caregiving

**Claude A. Mellins, Mindy J. Blum,
Sandra L. Boyd-Davis, and Margaret Gatz**

A n explosion of interest over the past 15 years has alerted gerontologists to the key role of family members as care providers for older adults with chronic mental and physical diseases. In turn, it has been suggested that those providing care are themselves at risk for both mental and physical distress. Any overview of mental health and aging must include this familial context when considering an elderly person's response to physical or mental changes.

Initially, studies focused on one family member, identified as the primary caregiver for the older adult. Typically this primary caregiver was the spouse—also elderly—or an adult daughter of the person needing assistance. Study samples were often recruited from membership lists of support organizations. A central research concern was the burden experienced by the caregiver. Most of this literature (summarized by Schulz, Visintainer and Williamson, 1990) found elevated scores on depressive symptom indices among caregivers, with rates of depression generally 30–50 percent. Since most studies used selected rather than representative samples, these rates may overstate risk.

Because the literature relies on selected samples, few data exist concerning the prevalence of family caregiving. A report from the House Select Committee on Aging (U.S. House of Representatives, 1987) suggests that the average American woman can expect to spend 18 years of her life helping a parent who has health impairments. Using a national data base, Stone and Kemper (1989) estimated that in the most vulnerable age group of adults—those 45–54 years old—odds were 1 out of 6 that a parent or spouse aged 65 or older would require some form of assistance. If one considers the risk to a given *family* that at least one older relative will need care, then odds of the family's being affected are even greater.

More recently, it has been suggested that several family members may be involved in caregiving and that the health decline of an elder touches multiple generations (Brody, 1989; Gatz, Bengtson and Blum, 1990). This alternative perspective is captured in the concept of "life event webs" (Pruchno, Blow and Smyer, 1984). These investigators argue that major life events have effects that radiate throughout the family, requiring adaptation in the family system, regardless of each individual's direct involvement with caregiving. Furthermore, families may experience multiple competing stresses, whose effects interact.

A family systems perspective reveals that duties may be shared with secondary caregivers (Brody, 1989; Pruchno, 1989). In addition, some empirical studies of "ripple effects" have been conducted. Brody (1989) offered examples of family members buffering or heightening the stress felt by primary caregivers. Similarly, Creasey and Jarvis (1989) found that children reported having a less supportive relationship with their fathers if their mothers were experiencing burden because of caring for a grandparent.

One recent theme in considering family network consequences of caregiving is the inclusion of both positive and negative effects. Studies have identified satisfactions or "uplifts" in addition to stresses experienced by primary caregivers (e.g., Kinney and Stephens, 1989). Others have suggested that caregivers may recognize their own personal growth and derive gratification from being able to care for a loved one (e.g., Motenko, 1989).

Our own research explores some of the implications of applying a family network perspective to caregiving. We interviewed 20 families, focusing on four questions: (1) Are caregiving responsibilities shared by multiple members of the family? (2) What are the physical and emotional consequences of caregiving? (3) Do caregiving activities result in altered relationships within the family? (4) Does exposure to the health decline of an elder result in changes in life perspective, either in terms of one's own development or views of other relatives?

Participants were part of an ongoing longitudinal survey study of families, including grandparent, parent, and grandchild generations (Bengtson and Roberts, 1991). Families were requested to participate in an additional interview if (a) at least one respondent identified a health impairment in an older relative, and (b) family members lived close enough to permit an in-person interview. The sample offers the advantage of representing a cross-section of caregiving issues to be expected in a population not initially selected for caregiving.

Sixty-two interviews were obtained: 14 care-recipients, 3 spouses of impaired elders, 19 adult children, 8 spouses of these adult children, and 18 adult grandchildren. Mean ages of the three generations were 84, 55, and 32 years, respectively.

In the 20 families, there were 23 care-recipients (in three families, both grandparents had health impairments). For the most part, care-recipients required considerable assistance with activities of daily living, including instrumental activities (e.g., shopping), mobility (e.g., walking up stairs), and self-care (e.g., bathing). Sixty-five percent of recipients were severely impaired in at least two of the three areas. Twelve recipients had primarily physical impairments (e.g., heart and blood pressure problems, severe arthritis), nine had predominantly cognitive impairments, and two showed both extensive physical and cognitive impairments. Eight of the 23 lived with family caregivers; two, in nursing homes; four, in retirement facilities; and nine, in their own homes. Both self-reports and caregivers' reports on the Activities of Daily Living Scale were obtained for the impaired elder. The interviewer or coder used other information from the interviews to resolve discrepancies.

A semistructured clinical interview was used, lasting an average of two hours. Formal content analysis of interview transcripts was conducted using coding categories developed to address the four study questions. Interrater reliability on 20 of the 62 interviews resulted in 81 percent concurrence on passage identification and coding classification of the passage.

SHARING OF CAREGIVING RESPONSIBILITIES

Each participant was asked to name everyone in the family involved in caregiving activities. Most families concurred on a primary caregiver. On average, however, three family members were substantially involved; in only one family was support limited to one person.

Examples of family division of caregiving tasks included the following: (1) two middle-aged siblings shared caregiving responsibilities—the son took care of at-home medical care and the daughter managed her parents' finances; (2) an elderly spouse provided extensive personal care for her husband, while her son and daughter-in-law were "on call" daily; and (3) a middle-aged married couple shared primary responsibilities for taking care of one of their parents, with their own adult child contributing to occasional shopping and transportation. One primary caregiver described the family response as "a team-type thing," with the work shared according to who was "available" and who was "willing."

PHYSICAL AND EMOTIONAL EFFECTS OF CAREGIVING

Family members reported anxiety, anger, guilt, and depression as a result of witnessing the health decline of a relative or the ensuing caregiving responsibilities. Emotional distress was not experienced only by primary caregivers. Both primary caregivers and other family members reported that they felt distressed; both also mentioned emotional stress they had observed in others. For example, one caregiver reported that her husband felt tension because they were both working and her parents were in need.

Caregiving often necessitated readjustments in social life; activities from attending civic meetings to dating were postponed or stopped. Some couples canceled vacations, others altered postretirement plans because of their parents' health problems.

Although less frequent, physical health effects such as weight loss, ulcers, and fatigue were noted. These effects were more commonly experienced by primary caregivers, while other relatives were often the source of the reports. For example, some grandchildren indicated concern about the physical impact of caregiving on their parents, who themselves were no longer young and healthy.

ALTERED RELATIONSHIPS WITHIN THE FAMILY

In each family, an average of four different dyadic relationships were described as affected by the elder's health-related dependency, going well beyond the relationship of the primary caregiver and care-recipient. Forty percent of references were of a positive nature; eight families reported more positive than negative changes. Positive changes typically involved increased closeness and social support among family members

40

who were contributing to the elder's care, as well as increased time spent together. For example, one adult daughter caregiving for her mother discussed her relationship with her own daughter: "One of the first times I felt really close to my daughter was when she helped me clean out my mother's apartment. It was very hard for both of us, but it was something we did together, and I really appreciated having a daughter."

However, not surprisingly, there were many references to negative effects. Eleven of the 20 families referred to more negative than positive altered relationships. The most common negative change was increased tension or conflict between primary caregivers and care-recipients, or between the primary caregivers and other family members who were less involved in helping, often precipitated by the perception that other family members were not "doing their fair share." Illustrating these negative effects, a middle-aged son noted that "the worst thing to come out of my mother's health problem" was family rifts and the intensification of disputes among "my uncle, my wife, and my mother." Additionally, several families noted competing demands stemming from the care needs of young children or from adult children "returning to the nest."

Other effects were not necessarily perceived as positive or negative: these included changes in family roles (e.g., a daughter feeling more like "the parent to her elderly father"), reallocation of family funds, and the content of family conversations (e.g., not discussing certain topics in order to protect the feelings of the elderly care-recipient).

ALTERED LIFE PERCEPTIONS

In 85 percent of the families, at least one person indicated a changed perspective about his or her place in the life cycle or about the nature of the family. The most frequent examples included recognizing one's own mortality, recognizing the mortality of one's parents and grandparents, and appreciating previously unrecognized strengths or vulnerabilities in one's parent or spouse. For example, an adult son indicated a fresh appreciation of the dedication of his mother who had not only raised her own children, but was now caregiving for her parent. One illustrative quote is from a 50-year old woman whose parents both had substantial health impairments: "I've got a few years behind me now, and with the birth of my grandchildren and my parents being in need, I can see the whole broad view of a person being born and dying."

41

Seventy percent of respondents who described a changed perspective were one step removed from daily contact with the elderly care-recipient. These respondents included adult grandchildren of the impaired elder, spouses of middle-aged caregivers, and middle-aged secondary caregivers (e.g., the adult child of an aging couple who were caring for each other). Possibly those who are somewhat removed from the caregiving situation have the time or emotional distance to reflect on its meaning. Although these family members may not be experiencing the daily strain of caregiving, they are not untouched by the experience of witnessing an elder's health decline and need for assistance.

CONCLUSION

The results described here illustrate the concept that caregiving is embedded in a "life event web" (Pruchno, Blow and Smyer, 1984), that life events not only affect those directly experiencing them but also other members of the family network, and that caregiving is superimposed on a fabric of ongoing family relationships. Consistent with comments by Suitor and Pillemer (1990), we found that there may not always be a clear demarcation of when caregiving begins. It is sometimes difficult to distinguish caregiving from the sorts of exchanges of assistance that would characterize family members' lifelong responsibilities.

Further demonstrating the contention that the caregiving situation should be regarded as a "family event" (Brody, 1989), in all but one family, several caregivers were identified, and relationships between multiple pairs of family members were altered by the caregiving situation. Although increased family tension was one common effect, it is noteworthy that—despite some instances of quite extensive caregiving responsibilities—changes were not exclusively negative. Rather, some families became closer and spent more time together.

Psychological effects of caregiving have typically been assessed in terms of a sense of burden or emotional distress, such as depression. We found that individuals also experience cognitive effects in the form of altered life perspectives (including reconceptualizations of "the meaning of life" and mortality) and altered views of other family members.

In summary, the present study illustrates the power of a family network perspective on caregiving. The data in this chapter reflect the interconnectedness of physical and mental health and the interconnection across generations: Changes in one family member can have diverse effects across multiple generations.

Acknowledgments

This research was supported by Grant No. 5 R37 AGO7977 from the National Institute on Aging, Vern L. Bengtson and Margaret Gatz (Principal Investigators). The authors thank Margo-Lea Hurwicz for her assistance with the interview protocol and data collection, also Donna Polisar for her help with data management.

References

Bengtson, V. L. and Roberts, R. E. L., 1991. "Intergenerational Solidarity in Aging Families: An Example of Formal Theory Construction." *Journal of Aging and the Family* 53: 856–70.

Brody, E. M., 1989. "The Family at Risk." In E. Light and B. D. Lebowitz, eds., *Alzheimer's Disease Treatment and Family Stress: Directions for Research.* Washington, DC: Government Printing Office, DHHS Publication No. (ADM) 89-1569, pp. 2–49.

Creasey, G. L. and Jarvis, P. A., 1989. "Grandparents with Alzheimer's Disease: Effects of Parental Burden." *Family Therapy* 16: 79–85.

Gatz, M., Bengtson, V. L. and Blum, M. J., 1990. "Caregiving Families." In J. E. Birren and K. W. Schaie, eds., *Handbook of the Psychology of Aging, 3rd ed.* San Diego, CA: Academic Press, pp. 404–26.

Kinney, J. M. and Stephens, M. A. P., 1989. "Hassles and Uplifts of Giving Care to a Family Member with Dementia." *Psychology and Aging* 4: 402–8.

Motenko, A. K., 1989. "The Frustration, Gratifications, and Well-Being of Dementia Caregivers." *Gerontologist* 29: 166–72.

Pruchno, R. A., 1989. "Alzheimer's Disease and Families: Methodological Advances." In E. Light and B. D. Lebowitz, eds., *Alzheimer's Disease Treatment and Family Stress: Directions for Research.* Washington, DC: Government Printing Office, DHHS Publication No. (ADM) 89-1569, pp. 2–49.

Pruchno, R. A., Blow, F. C. and Smyer, M. A., 1984. "Life Events and Interdependent Lives." *Human Development* 27: 31–41.

Schulz, R., Visintainer, P. and Williamson, G. M., 1990. "Psychiatric and Physical Morbidity Effects of Caregiving." *Journal of Gerontology*:

Psychological Sciences 45: 181–91.

Stone, R. and Kemper, P., 1989. "Spouses and Children of Disabled Elders: How Large a Constituency for Long-Term Care Reform?" *Milbank Quarterly*, 67: 485–506.

Suitor, J. J. and Pillemer, K., 1990. "Transition to the Status of Family Caregiver: A New Framework for Studying Social Support and Well-Being." In S. M. Stahl, ed., *The Legacy of Longevity: Health and Health Care in Later Life.* Newbury Park, CA: Sage.

U. S. House of Representatives, Select Committee on Aging, Subcommittee on Human Services, 1987. *Exploding the Myths: Caregiving in America.* Washington, DC: Government Printing Office, Comm. Pub. No. 99-611.

Mental Health and Aging

A Decade of Progress

Sanford I. Finkel

ith the myriad difficulties confronting the field of geriatric mental health, it is easy to overlook the fact that considerable progress has been made over the past 10 years. One impetus for many positive developments was the 1981 White House Conference on Aging, as well as the Miniconference on Mental Health of Older Americans, which preceded the 1981 conference. The miniconference represented a joint effort by the American Nurses Association, the American Psychiatric Association, the American Psychological Association, and the National Association of Social Workers. Over a hundred representatives of professional organizations, lay organizations, governmental agencies, and consumer groups assembled to evaluate the impact of research, finances, services, and training in meeting the mental healthcare needs of the nation's elderly. One goal of the miniconference was to provide timely and practical information on mental health in the elderly to the representatives of the White House Conference on Aging. Another goal was to improve the quality of interaction among groups concerned with mental health and the elderly, including organizations of elderly, legislative/policy staff, and geriatric healthcare specialists who treat elderly with mental health needs.

A number of key recommendations from this miniconference were included in the report from the 1981 White House Conference on Aging itself. Further, several significant recommendations have become realities, either by law or by policy. If there is to be another White House Conference on Aging, we can anticipate additional impetus for a greater understanding of the mental health needs of older Americans and for policies directed at fulfilling them.

Anticipating another conference, an interdisciplinary coordinating group on mental health in the elderly assembled in early 1992 to review the past decade, to assess the current status of the field, and to project developments in the future. Representatives of this group were from the American Nursing Association (Celeste Dye and May Wykle), the American Psychiatric Association (Sanford Finkel and Donald Hay), the American Psychological Association (Margaret Gatz and Michael Smyer), and the National Association of Social Workers (Alejandro Garcia and Roberta Greene). This chapter represents a summary of our efforts. Since some of the group's substantive areas are discussed elsewhere in this volume (e.g., special populations and organization of services), they will not be considered in this chapter. Instead, the focus will be on six key areas: financing, research, public information and prevention, intergenerational issues, long-term care, and training and education.

The period 1982–1992 was one of accomplishment, continued problems, and opportunities in the above-mentioned six key areas.

FINANCING

A number of positive financial developments have occurred over the past decade. The $250 cap on outpatient mental healthcare under Medicare Part B was increased under the Omnibus Budget Reconciliation Act of 1987 (OBRA 87). The cap was repealed altogether under OBRA 89. In addition, Medicare now pays directly for qualified mental healthcare services provided by clinical psychologists and clinical social workers. It is expected that Congress will continue to expand Medicare coverage of services provided by other mental healthcare providers. Further, benefits have improved and services have increased for home healthcare, occupational therapy, and some outpatient services. Comprehensive assessment for people with mental disorders in long-term-care facilities has also expanded significantly. The establishment of tax incentives for family caregiving is beginning, a phenomenon that should grow over the next decade, given the enormous economic costs associated with some of the very late life illnesses (Biegel et al., 1986).

In long-term-care settings, OBRA 87 has substantially mandated training for and upgrading of mental health services provided. Finally, research funding for the Center for Mental Disorders of the Aging of the National Institute of Mental Health (NIMH), as well as for the National Institute on Aging (NIA), has substantially increased over this past decade. However, such funding is still at a level substantially below expenditures for research in other areas.

Financial pressures spurred by high hospital costs should result in a decline in hospitalization and an increasing utilization of partial hospitalization and community treatment for older psychiatric patients. The primary goal is to reduce the need for inpatient settings, a trend that has been marked in nongeriatric populations.

In response to OBRA 90, the National Association of Insurance Commissioners recently revised the model Medicare Supplemental (Medigap) insurance regulation governing Medigap insurance, which all states must implement. Revised model regulations require that all Medigap policies cover the 50 percent coinsurance for outpatient mental healthcare under Medicare Part B. This change promises to help offset the cost of this care. However, the change is prospective and will therefore not apply to older adults holding Medigap policies in effect prior to their state's adoption of the new model regulation.

The developments are all signs of progress. On the other hand, much remains to be accomplished.

Outpatient mental healthcare is still subject to the discriminatory 50 percent copayment. This statutory requirement applies in nursing home settings as well. Thus, it is not surprising that payments for psychiatric services account for only 2.4 percent of all Medicare reimbursements. Moreover, in 1989, Congress adopted a new Resource-Based Relative Value Scale (RBRVS) methodology to determine payment under the national Medicare fee schedule for physician and other healthcare services. The RBRVS fee schedule poses unique problems for psychiatry—and concomitantly for psychology and social work, whose fees are linked to those for psychiatry. In brief, current payment rules create barriers and disincentives to the provision of needed mental healthcare, particularly to residents in nursing facilities.

With the advent of a prospective payment system using diagnosis-related groups under Medicare, over a third of public mental health agencies studied indicated a change in their clientele, with a higher percentage being more frail and sick and in need of more case services (Wood and Estes, 1990).

There remains a 190-day lifetime cap for treatment in private psychiatric hospitals. This also applies to free-standing public hospitals, but not to psychiatric units of general hospitals. Certain sources of rising healthcare costs, including administration, "defensive medicine," and malpractice insurance, have been only nominally or minimally addressed. A growing number of states are experiencing fiscal difficulties, significantly affecting their delivery of healthcare services, particularly their mental healthcare systems and services.

As healthcare costs continue to escalate, there is more discussion of implementation of healthcare rationing. Recently, in fact, the Oregon State Legislature voted to limit Medicaid to a predetermined per capita spending level with specific limitations for expensive treatment of certain illnesses— for example, open heart surgery and hemodialysis (Brown, 1991; Fox and Leichter, 1991). Healthcare reform proposals to deal with these problems are abundant and are being debated in Congress though none has been adopted to date.

The need for private long-term-care insurance is becoming increasingly apparent to many adults in their 50s and 60s. Although such programs are increasingly in demand and although privatization is consistent with government planning and needs, most policies have provisions that exclude mental illness, including dementias. Currently, no firm standards are in place that would allow coverage for these illnesses.

One final point: Perhaps as much as 23 percent of healthcare cost is spent on mental illness—for example, for treatment of anxiety and depression—yet most of the services are not provided by mental health professionals. Further, we pay for patients with mental health problems in nursing homes, but not specifically for mental health services. Rather, we pay for the effects of not providing mental health services.

RESEARCH

The past decade has witnessed the mainstreaming of gerontological and geriatric research. Extraordinary advances have taken place in neuroscience, in understanding the mechanisms of cognitive and intellectual function, and in social network theory. Improved methodology has facilitated the examination of increasingly complex models in a variety of disciplines and has led to improved integration of disciplines. Such developments are necessary to more fully understand biological, psychological, psychosocial, and clinical aspects of mental health and mental illness. As a result, a broader understanding of the difference between aging (a process that goes on) and old age (a context that brings disease) has begun to emerge.

Federal support for research activities from NIA and NIMH has substantially increased during this decade. The additional support has included clinical research centers for geriatric mental health, as well as NIMH centers for depression. Further, funding via private foundations and pharmaceutical companies for research activities involving older people has grown considerably. Research activities have also been encouraged by the Zenith Award (Alzheimer's Association), the International Psychogeriatric Association (IPA) Research Awards in Psychogeriatrics (Miles Inc., Pharmaceutical Division), and the Gerontological Research Awards (Sandoz).

The intellectual challenges in studying mental illnesses and normal aging processes of late life have led to a considerable increase in participation in the field by scientists. As a result, research interest and grant applications by scientists and researchers at all levels of experience and training have markedly increased.

The Epidemiological Catchment Area surveys, and the World Health Organization's initiatives in the area of research on depression and dementia have contributed to our understanding of the epidemiology of dementias and other psychiatric disorders, and have significantly added to our knowledge base.

Especially encouraging has been the enormous increase in research on Alzheimer's disease and other dementias, which has provided enhanced understanding of the genetics, neurochemistry, diagnosis, and management aspects of this devastating illness. The establishment of the Consortium for Establishment of a Registry for Alzheimer's Disease has helped to develop sites with special research expertise.

Growing attention has also been paid to the onset of major psychiatric disorders, including schizophrenia and depressive disorders, with results suggesting that the course of these illnesses varies depending on age of onset and outcome of early treatment (Miller and Cohen, 1987).

Research on treatment of acute depressive episodes in later life has shown high degrees of recovery using medications and psychotherapy, although relapse and recurrence are common.

As our research efforts yield specific information on diagnosis and treatment, clinicians have increasingly been able to translate these findings to patients and their families. In turn, they provide feedback to researchers, validating or negating the research findings. This process provides valuable information to the researchers and directs the course of clinical investigation, thereby generating new hypotheses.

On the other hand, minimal meaningful research has been completed on personality disorders, anxiety, delirium, chronic mental illness, or mental retardation in later life. Areas of "soft" research have lagged behind biological research. These areas include research on the effectiveness of psychotherapies, prevention, adjustment disorders of late life, evaluation of health services, understanding quality-of-life issues involved in mental illness in later life, intergenerational issues, normal personality development, assessment of effects of culture and economics on later life mental health, and bioethical issues. Research on pharmacodynamics and chemical dependencies has also lagged compared to other areas. Finally, research on suicide in late life has also been minimal, even though the already high rates of late-life suicide soared between 1980 and 1986 (Meehan, Saltzman and Sattin, 1991).

Closer collaboration is needed to link NIA and NIMH funding with the Administration on Aging funding priorities. There is the potential danger that competition between and among federal agencies could impair certain research efforts. Agreement on how best to share interests and expertise while pooling funding is very much needed on both federal and state levels.

PUBLIC INFORMATION AND PREVENTION

Education, public information, and prevention were principal themes in the 1981 White House Conference on Aging. We have seen many advances in these areas over the past decade. Many voluntary and lay organizations have taken an active role in educating older people and their family members on a host of topics related to mental health and aging: NIA has put out an *Age Page;* NIMH has produced *Fact Sheets* on several issues; the American Association of Retired Persons (AARP) has developed a variety of reports on topics, including the use of psychotropic medications, suicide in late life, and alcoholism; and the National Council on the Aging (NCOA) has offered many programs to enhance the quality of life.

AARP also formed its Coalition on Mental Health and Aging in 1981. Its principal goals include educating industry/business and labor, policy makers, consumers, and the media regarding issues related to mental health and aging. (Larry Rickards describes the coalition and its current work in chapter 19.)

The effects of public education and prevention efforts are apparent in a variety of population indicators. The prevalence of atherosclerotic disease, including myocardial infarctions and cerebrovascular accidents, has been on the decline. Decreased smoking, better weight control, lower cholesterol levels, and increased exercise have all contributed to a healthier older population. Further, there is a tendency toward earlier intervention for high-risk populations. For example, spouses of people with dementia are prone toward developing major depression, which early intervention could well prevent. Mental health intervention has also been shown to be helpful in decreasing excess disability caused by physical illness (Mumford, Schlesinger and Glass, 1982).

The past decade has seen a marked change in the media treatment of older people, who are now depicted in a more sensitive and humane fashion. The media have also improved in their provision of factual information about late life changes. Newspapers, movies, and television have all contributed to this changing image. Hospitals and agencies have devoted more time and effort to educating older people regarding their health and well-being. Formal educational programs for the elderly exist in one-third of the 3,000 colleges and universities in the United States, reflecting older adults' increasing demand for higher educational services.

In contrast, knowledge of memory function including potentials for memory enhancement have been neglected, in spite of the evidence that techniques used in the classroom setting or by computer can partially mitigate certain symptoms of age-associated cognitive decline (Yesavage, 1985; Finkel and Yesavage, 1989).

Moreover, little has been done to encourage an intergenerational focus, though intergenerational daycare centers have slowly begun to be developed. Older people themselves have not been enlisted in prevention/public information efforts, so an important potential asset has been neglected.

One challenge for the future is evaluation of programmatic interventions. The effectiveness of information campaigns and prevention programs must also be assessed.

INTERGENERATIONAL ISSUES

Intergenerational issues will be a central theme for the next White House Conference on Aging. Among the purposes of the proposed conference are the following: (1) to increase the public awareness of the interdependence of generations and the essential contributions of older individuals to society for the well-being of all generations, (2) to identify the problems facing older individuals and the commonalities of the problems of younger generations, and (3) to review the status and intergenerational value of recommendations adopted at previous White House Conferences on Aging. This emphasis is in contrast to the 1981 White House Conference on Aging, in which intergenerational issues garnered few specific recommendations.

There have been several positive developments in the area of intergenerational issues over the past decade. Thanks in large part to the Alzheimer's Association, caregivers of people with dementia have progressively received more interest and focus. This has resulted in increasing services and care.

Intergenerational projects, though still limited, are expanding. Both the older person and the younger person benefit from their mutual participation. Current programs include efforts like Magic Me in Baltimore, in which middle-school children visit nursing homes, and Lifetimes, in which older volunteers assist unwed mothers or middle-school youngsters with behavioral problems or juvenile delinquency. The NCOA has long supported a foster grandparent program. A similar NCOA program involves high school and college students visiting nursing homes.

Increasing attention has also been accorded to the provision of eldercare services for working adult children who have older parents that are ill. This has been spurred by industry, especially by IBM. Adult children over 40 who have a mentally or physically sick older parent requiring care are more apt to experience absenteeism, tardiness, and cessation of employment owing to stress and mental disorders, including anxiety and depression. Although the troubled economy has slowed the growth of this benefit, which provides education, information and referral, and self-help groups, there is a clear trend toward the delivery of eldercare services within industry. Further, there has been increased information available to caregivers (e.g., Briar and Kaplan, 1990).

A study sponsored by AARP (1987) on intergenerational tension revealed the following results: few signs of intergenerational tension, evidence of mutual respect and concern from generation to generation, an ongoing commitment to the value of family responsibility, and continued support for an active social role for government. The tension in society, the report argued, was linked not so much to age but rather to educational attainment and income.

Despite progress, a number of vexing problems remain:

- Supplemental Security Income is reduced if an elderly person lives in a relative's home.
- With shrinking financial resources, there is indeed some competition between the generations.
- Services should be conceptualized as dyadic- or family-based, as opposed to the usual individual-based conceptualization.
- Better epidemiological information encompassing family structure and function is needed.
- More research is needed in defining intergenerational issues, including the evolution of four- and five-generation families.

LONG-TERM CARE

The major event of the decade in long-term care was the passage of OBRA 87. Among its provisions were the following:

- Mandating that mental health services be available within the nursing home, or from an outside agency. This has increased the number of available mental health professionals providing nursing home services, inasmuch as psychologists and social workers now are reimbursed by Medicare.

- Increasing in-service and other training for staff.
- Emphasizing improvement of the quality of life in the nursing home.
- More careful tracking of key factors in the older person's life, part-

ly by attention to a Minimum Data Set (Morris et al., 1991), which tracks a variety of important variables, including cognitive, behavioral, and psychiatric functioning.

• Increasing specialized services for elderly nursing home residents with primary mental illness.

There has also been a tendency for university settings to establish relationships with "teaching nursing homes" and thus expand the quality of clinical services while providing excellent educational opportunities.

Finally, the number of board and care homes increased for those who do not require healthcare assistance on site, although there is some concern about the quality of care in these underregulated settings.

Nevertheless, many aspects of long-term care still need attention. Twenty-three percent of the over-age-85 population now requires nursing home care, and nursing homes continue to remain significantly underserved by mental health professionals, partly as a result of financial disincentives.

There are few models of comprehensive mental health services in the nursing home environment, though OBRA 87 may encourage their development. However, OBRA 87 has further increased the costliness of nursing homes, and the affordability of a good nursing home is becoming a greater problem for more older Americans.

Inasmuch as the vast majority of nursing home residents have mental disorders (Rovner et al., 1986), those discharged from the nursing home risk becoming the elderly homeless.

There is a paucity of research in the nursing home setting. This sometimes leads—as in the case with the effort to reduce use of psychotropic drugs—to sweeping government policy without a scientific factual basis regarding how to proceed.

TRAINING AND EDUCATION

Over the past decade, major new developments in training and education—developments that seemed unlikely, if not impossible, in 1982—have taken place. Examinations were established for "added qualifications" in geriatric medicine (beginning in 1988) and geriatric psychiatry (beginning in 1991). These are not specialty examinations but rather verify the accumulation of a specialized knowledge of the field and encourage generalists to develop special expertise for their elderly patients. Moreover, fellowship programs have been established. In geriatric psychiatry, for example, over 40 programs currently offer this advanced training, in contrast to one such program only 15 years ago.

Further, increasing curriculum attention has been accorded to geriatric mental health in all disciplines. Increasing emphasis during the basic programs in the professional schools is placed on knowledge, skills, and attitudes critical to providing mental health services to older people.

Initiatives for geriatric and gerontological education emanate from several federal sources. Multidisciplinary geriatric education centers have been established. The Veterans Administration has begun educational programs in geriatrics and gerontology. The Geriatric Academic Mental Health Awards and other such training awards have been created and sponsored by the NIA and NIMH.

There has also been rapid growth and dissemination of information in the field as exemplified by the following: (1) Although few textbooks were available on geriatric mental health 15 years ago, seven are in circulation today (Jacoby and Oppenheimer, 1991; Bienenfeld, 1990; Busse and Blazer, 1980; Birren and Sloane, 1980; Butler, Lewis and Sunderland, 1991). In addition, myriad other highly specialized books are available. (2) In contrast to only one specialty journal or newsletter in the field 15 years ago, eight exist today. (3) Meetings on geriatric mental health, which were few and far between 15 years ago, are commonplace today. The American Association of Geriatric Psychiatry holds an annual meeting, and the IPA holds a biennial congress. More general meetings in geriatrics, gerontology, and psychiatry pay increasing attention to geriatric mental health issues. (4) The federal government has sponsored several important conferences, including the NIH Consensus Conference on Depression (1992), and NIMH conferences and workshops on late-life anxiety (1989), schizophrenia (1982), suicide (1992), and the use of psychotropic medication in nursing homes (1992).

There are continued problems in this area, however. With the rapidly expanding population, more faculty are needed. There is a dearth of programs with several key faculty members in geriatric mental health. Further, interdisciplinary cross-fertilization needs to accelerate. A core curriculum also needs to be developed for each profession, with outcome measures established. Finally, more efficient ways must be developed for organizing the massive amount of information and data that is besieging clinicians and researchers working in the field.

CONCLUSION

Because so many shortages and problems exist in our society, it is easy to focus on the part of the glass that is empty. In order to maintain our own sense of hopefulness, however, it is critical that sometimes we remind ourselves of how far we have come. Certainly, the rapid growth in the numbers of the very old, the financial problems that face our society, and the current state of our knowledge base in treating certain major mental disorders of late life continue to confound and challenge us. Nevertheless, substantial changes in the understanding of mental health and aging have occurred over the past decade. These changes have transpired in a rapidly changing policy context.

We have started this decade stronger in several ways than we were in the 1980s. Our federal research resources are larger. Far more attention is being paid to outcome, and an enhanced interest in working models of service delivery is evident. We have come a long way in education, and have made some inroads in long-term care. Yet we have seriously lagged behind in efforts with special populations, including the elderly minority subgroups, and intergenerational issues are only beginning to emerge for study and attention. In the best of all worlds, creative funding mechanisms will develop that correspond to our increasing clinical understanding of the mentally ill older adult. The next White House Conference on Aging, whenever it occurs, will provide another opportunity to consider these issues and to chart future progress. Optimally, creative financial directions will evolve in a way that corresponds to our increasing clinical understanding of the individual.

References

American Association of Retired Persons, 1987. *Intergenerational Tension in 1987: Real or Imagined?* Washington, DC.

Biegel, B. E. et al., 1986. *Family Care Incentive Policies.* Final Report to the Pennsylvania Department of Aging.

Bienenfeld, D., ed., 1990. *Verwoerdt's Clinical Geropsychiatry, 3rd ed.* Baltimore, MD: Williams and Wilkins.

Birren, J. E. and Sloane, R. B., 1980. *Handbook of Mental Health and Aging.*

Englewood Cliffs, NJ: Prentice-Hall.

Briar, K. H. and Kaplan, C., 1990. *The Family Caregiving Crisis.* Silver Spring, MD: National Association of Social Workers.

Brown, L. D., 1991. "The National Politics of Oregon's Rationing Plan." *Health Affairs* 10: 28–51.

Busse, E. W. and Blazer, D., eds. 1980. *Handbook of Geriatric Psychiatry.* New York: Van Nostrand.

Butler, R., Lewis, M. I. and Sunderland, T., 1991. *Aging and Mental Health: Positive Psychosocial and Biomedical Approaches, 4th ed.* New York: Merrill

Finkel, S., Lyons, J. and Anderson, R., 1993. "A Brief Agitation Rating Scale (BARS) for Nursing Home Elderly." *Journal of the American Geriatric Society* 41(1): 50–52.

Finkel, S. I. and Yesavage, J. A., 1989. "Learning Mnemonics: A Preliminary Evaluation of a Computer-Aided Instruction Package for the Elderly." *Journal of Experimental Aging Research* 15(3-4): 199–202.

Flemming, A. S. et al., 1986. Report on a Survey of Community Mental Health Centers, Washington, DC: Action Committee to Implement the Mental Health Recommendations of the 1981 White House Conference on Aging.

Fox, D. M. and Leichter, H. M., 1991. "Rationing Care in Oregon: The New Accountability." *Health Affairs* 10: 7–27.

Jacoby, R. and Oppenheimer, C., eds., 1991. *Psychiatry in the Elderly.* Oxford, UK: Oxford University Press.

Meehan, P. J., Saltzman, L. E. and Sattin, R. W., 1991. "Suicide Among Older United States Residents: Epidemiologic Characteristics and Trends." *American Journal of Public Health* 81: 1187–1200.

Miller, N. and Cohen, G., 1987. *Schizophrenia and Aging.* New York: Guilford Press.

Morris, J. N. et al., 1991. *Minimum Data Set—Resident Assessment Instrument Training Manual and Resource Guide.* Natick, MA: Eliot Press.

Mumford, E., Schlesinger, H. J. and Glass, G. V., 1982. "The Effects of Psychological Intervention on Recovery from Surgery and Heart Attacks: An Analysis of the Literature." *American Journal of Public Health* 172: 141–57.

Rovner, M. et al., 1986. "Prevalence of Mental Illness in a Community Nursing Home." *American Journal of Psychiatry* 143: 1446–49.

Wood, J. B. and Estes, C. L., 1990. "The Impact of DRGs on Community-Based Service Providers: Implications for the Elderly." *American Journal of Public Health* 80: 840–43.

Yesavage, J. A., 1985. "Nonpharmacologic Treatments for Memory Losses with Normal Aging." *American Journal of Psychiatry* 142: 600–605.

An Optimistic View of the Aging Brain

Marian Cleeves Diamond

W e hope to grow old; yet we dread old age" wrote La Bruyère in the seventeenth century. Hazlitt, in the nineteenth century, came more to the point with, "The worst old age is that of the brain " But as we approach the twenty-first century and use some of the knowledge gained from controlled experimental animal data and from healthy old human brains, we can begin to be a little less pessimistic and more optimistic about the potential of the aging brain.

In early aging-brain studies, investigators did not always use brains from active, well, old human beings; they used any brains that were available for study. Even today, many researchers do not separate the process of aging from the effects of environmental isolation. Animals kept in solitary conditions for years do not represent normal aging. Their brains should not be examined as products of normal aging. We have shown in the laboratory how readily isolation can cause brain cells in the cerebral cortex to shrink.

Let us stop for a moment and consider more closely this incomparable organ to which we have been referring. How many people actually think about their own brains? I mean really appreciate the magnitude of the potential of these 100 billion cells housed within their heads? The three-pound mass of tissue called the human brain is the most complex mass of protoplasm on this earth—perhaps even in our galaxy. It is the product of both heredity and environment operative for many millions

59

of years, yet its potential is still virtually unknown. This organ can conceive of a universe a billion light years or more across or can create ideas nonexistent in previous moments. Only the brain can inform us about our universe. The brain and its expressions are unique for every individual who has ever lived. This is the best lesson in self-respect we can offer anyone.

Thus, the knowledge shared here will come in a different order for every individual, depending on the variety of encounters with that individual's reality. No two readers will be interpreting these words identically. How important for those of us in education to keep this in mind!

How much influence does the brain have in controlling its own destiny during aging? On one hand, it can predict the negative sides of its fate with more dementia, more illness, and more social problems over the years and decades ahead. Similarly, by examining the structural, functional, and biochemical alterations occurring during abnormal aging, we can better understand the changes in the macromolecular composition and turnover of brain cells, regulation of gene expression, DNA and RNA synthesis, qualitative and quantitative changes of synaptosomal plasma membrane proteins, diminished plasticity, and so on.

On the other hand, we can use the information that offers a more positive view of the aging brain, after examining some of the more favorable facts about its potential, to create a more optimistic path toward the process of living a long, healthy life. After all, the brain does play a role in controlling the aging process of the body just as the body plays such a role in controlling the aging brain—an aging circle. Plato recognized this fact in 400 B. C.

When one speaks of old age, one commonly refers to the chronological age of the total individual, not necessarily the biological age of the various cellular constituents. The processes of development and aging are occurring simultaneously in various parts of the body during a total lifetime. During fetal development, it has been reported, nerve cells are forming at the rate of 50,000 per second. Before a baby is born, it has already lost at least 50 percent of the nerve cells in its brain. This is because more nerve cells are produced than are needed. Since nerve cells as a rule do not divide after being formed, an overproduction exists. Those that make functional connections survive; those that do not, die. What we do not know, however, is whether we could prevent some of this brain cell loss. For example, could we prevent such loss in the developing fetal brain by "enriching" the pregnant rats? If we could, then what would be the advantage to the animals' behavior of having more nerve cells in the brain?

Now let us consider some of the experimental data where we have been able to control a few of the many variables impinging upon a mammalian body as we study the development and aging of brains (Diamond, 1988). The majority of our studies have been carried out on the anatomy of the forebrain of a lower mammal, the rat, for the following reasons: (1) rats have large litters, so the genetic background is somewhat controlled; (2) rats are bright, intelligent animals; (3) they are small, clean animals, and we can control their diet and their environmental conditions; and most important for our studies, (4) they have a smooth cerebral cortex, which is relatively easy to measure, unlike the folded cortices of higher mammals.

What have we learned from 30 years of studying the effects of enriched and impoverished environments on the cerebral cortex? We have learned that we can change the structure of this complex mass of brain tissue at any age, either by increasing or decreasing the dimension of its nerve cells or the number of the glial cells.

What are the environmental living conditions that allow such changes to take place? In the "enriched condition," 12 rats live together in a large cage about one meter square, and they have access to objects to explore. In the "standard condition," three rats live together in a small cage, roughly one foot square, with no objects to explore. In the "impoverished condition," only one rat lives in a small cage, about one foot square, with no objects. After the rats live in these conditions for different time periods and at different ages, the brains are examined. With enriched conditions, the cerebral cortex increases its thickness compared to the brains from animals living in standard conditions. With an impoverished condition, the cerebral cortex decreases its thickness.

What does a thickness change mean? Brains are made of nerve cells, glial cells, and blood vessels. In our experiments we have learned that every part of the nerve cell, from soma to dendrites to dendritic spines to synapses, alters its dimensions in response to the environment. The enlarged nerve cells demand more glial cell support and larger capillaries. This combination of cells and blood supply is apparently utilized by the rats to solve maze problems more effectively than rats without such modifications. The mechanism by which the enlarged nerve cells improve learning ability is not yet known, but these findings clearly demonstrate brain enlargement as a result of brain use.

Just as the cortical neurons become larger in a stimulating environment, they decrease in size when there is less input from the millions of sensory receptors reporting from the body surface and the internal organs. It is just as important to stress the fact that decreased stimulation will diminish a nerve cell's dendrites as it is to stress that increased stimulation will enlarge the dendritic tree. We have seen how readily the cortical thickness diminishes with an impoverished environment, and, at times, the negative effects of impoverishment are of greater magnitude than the positive effects brought about by a comparable period of enrichment.

Perhaps the single most valuable piece of information learned from all our studies is that structural differences can be detected in the cerebral cortices of animals exposed at any age to different levels of stimulation in the environment. First, we found that young animals placed in enriched environments just after weaning developed measurable changes in cortical morphology (Diamond, Krech and Rosenzweig, 1964). Then, we worked backward in age to animals not yet weaned and found such changes (Malkasian and Diamond, 1971), and we even found measurable effects of prenatal enrichment. Later, we moved forward in age to learn that the enriched young adult rat demonstrated an increase in dendritic growth, not only above that found in his impoverished mates, but even above the level of the standard colony animals (Uylings et al., 1979). In the very old animal, with the cortex following its normal decline with aging, we again found the enriched cortex significantly thicker than the nonenriched (Diamond et al., 1985).

At every age studied, we have shown anatomical effects due to enrichment or impoverishment. The results from enriched animals provide a degree of optimism about the potential of the brain in elderly human beings, just as the effects of impoverishment warn us of the deleterious consequence of inactivity.

The ultimate goal of all of our studies has been to gain a better understanding of human behavior by examining its source, the brain. Now how do we apply this knowledge for the benefit of people? Since no two human brains are exactly alike, no enriched environment will completely satisfy any two individuals for an extended period of time.

The range of enriched environments for human beings is endless. For some, interacting with objects is gratifying; for others, obtaining information is rewarding; and for still others, working with creative ideas is most enjoyable. But no matter what form enrichment takes, it is the challenge to the nerve cells that is important.

In one experiment where the rats could watch other rats "play" with their toys but could not play themselves, the brains of the observer rats did not show measurable changes (Furchman, Bennett and Rosenzweig, 1975). These data indicate that passive observation is not enough; one must interact with the environment.

One way to be certain of continued enrichment is to maintain curiosity throughout a lifetime. Always asking questions of yourself or others and in turn seeking out the answers provides continual changes to nerve cells. The basic message is, "Use it or lose it."

Acknowledgments

This chapter is adapted from the Sol Kramer Lecture, delivered in 1989 to the College of Health and Human Development, Pennsylvania State University, University Park.

References

Diamond, M. C., 1988. *Enriching Heredity.* New York: Free Press.

Diamond, M. C., Krech, D. and Rosenzweig, M. R., 1964. "The Effects of an Enriched Environment on the Histology of the Rat Cerebral Cortex." *Journal of Comparative Neurology* 123: 111–20.

Diamond, M.C. et al., 1985. "Plasticity in the 904-Day-Old Rat." *Experimental Neurology* 87: 309–17.

Furchman, P A., Bennett, E. and Rosenzweig, M. R., 1975. "Direct Contact with Enriched Environment Required to Alter Cerebral Weights in Rats." *Journal of Comparative Physiology and Psychology* 88: 360–67.

Malkasian, D. and Diamond, M.C., 1971. "The Effect of Environmental Manipulation on the Morphology of the Neonatal Rat Brain." *International Journal of Neuroscience* 2: 161–70.

Uylings, H. B. H. et al., 1979. "Dendritic Outgrowth in the Visual Cortex of Adult Rats Under Different Environmental Conditions." *Experimental Neurology* 62: 658–77.

Depressive Disorders and Symptoms in Later Life

Linda K. George

nlike many physical illnesses, most psychiatric disorders lack objective, easily measured markers. Thermometers, sphygmomanometers, X-rays, and similar technologies are largely irrelevant to psychiatric diagnosis. Instead, mental illnesses are diagnosed on the basis of symptoms reported by patients and observed by clinicians. Because there are no objective markers for psychiatric disorders, conceptual models of the ways symptoms combine to form meaningful diagnostic categories are especially important. The purpose of this chapter is to provide an overview of the two major conceptualizations of depression in the clinical and research literatures on psychiatric morbidity. These models are defined, and their relative strengths and weaknesses are assessed. Distinctive features of late-life depression are highlighted, and it is shown that studies of geriatric depression pose challenges to the dominant conceptual models of depressive disorder. The final section briefly reconsiders the role of conceptual models in mental health research and practice and suggests high-priority topics for future inquiry.

DEPRESSION AS A PSYCHIATRIC DISORDER

The official diagnostic classification of psychiatric disorders is the American Psychiatric Association's *Diagnostic and Statistical Manual of Mental Disorders* (abbreviated DSM). Two versions of this manual have guided psychiatric practice for the last decade: DSM-III and DSM-III-R (APA, 1980, 1987). DSM-III and DSM-III-R are the conceptual foundations of psychiatric diagnosis in the United States. Developed by psychiatrists, DSM diagnostic criteria are used by the broad range of mental health professionals and third-party payers (such as Medicare and private insurance plans).

There are multiple depressive disorders, with DSM-III and DSM-III-R providing nearly identical definitions. When scientists and clinicians discuss "clinical depression," they are referring to the specific diagnosis of major depression. Subcategories of major depression are based on whether or not the individual also exhibits psychotic features, exhibits significant symptoms of melancholia, or experiences a seasonal pattern of depression. Episodes of major depression are also observed in bipolar disorder, characterized by both manic and depressive phases. Because bipolar disorder is a distinct illness, with unique risk factors, course, and appropriate treatments, it will not be considered further here.

Major depression is the most common depressive disorder and the focus of most research on geriatric depression. However, the DSM-III and DSM-III-R diagnostic systems include two additional depressive disorders. Dysthymia is more chronic but less severe than major depression and is often referred to as depressive neurosis. A residual diagnosis exists for depressive syndromes that do not meet the criteria for major depression or dysthymia; this disorder is called atypical depression in DSM-III and a depressive disorder not otherwise specified in DSM-III-R.

DSM-III and DSM-III-R guidelines define depressive disorders in terms of multiple criteria. First, the individual must exhibit the required number of symptoms of the disorder. Depressive symptoms include feelings of sadness, loss of appetite, excessive weight loss or gain, sleep disturbances, fatigue, restlessness, loss of interest in daily activities, trouble concentrating, feelings of guilt or worthlessness, thoughts of death, a desire to die, and suicide attempts. Five or more symptoms are required for a diagnosis of major depression. Second, the clinician must conclude that the symptoms are of psychogenic origin rather than resulting from physical illness or the use of medication, illicit drugs, or alcohol. The symptoms also must be severe, must persist for a minimum of two weeks, and must occur together, forming a syndromal episode.

DSM-III and DSM-III-R have several strengths when compared to previous diagnostic systems. First, there is substantial evidence that the criteria for these systems can be applied reliably by mental health professionals, in contrast to previous systems (George et al., 1989). Second, the criteria define relatively homogeneous groups of patients from whom research results on risk factors and treatment efficacy can be generalized. Third, depressive disorders are defined solely on the basis of signs and symptoms. This basis is important for (1) etiologic research, because the measure of disease is not confounded with potential risk factors, and (2) validation research, because evidence about course, outcome, and treatment response is obtained independently of evidence used to make the diagnosis.

DEPRESSION AS A CONTINUUM OF SYMPTOMS

Using diagnostic criteria, individuals are evaluated as either having or not having depressive disorder. An alternative to this dichotomous approach is to view depression as a continuum, with individuals' places on the continuum determined by the number of symptoms experienced during a defined period of time. A variety of standardized scales exist for measuring depressive symptoms (e.g., Radloff, 1977; Yesavage et al., 1983). Note that in addition to yielding continuous measures, symptom scales also ignore other criteria that are used in making psychiatric diagnoses (e.g., severity, duration). When such scales are used in population surveys, a significant minority of respondents report no depressive symptoms, the majority report small numbers of symptoms, and a very small proportion report large numbers of symptoms (e.g., Eaton and Kessler, 1981; Mirowsky and Ross, 1989).

Whether depression is conceptualized as a psychiatric disorder or as a continuum of symptoms has important implications. One conceptual framework is not uniformly superior to the other; rather, choice of a conceptual orientation should be determined by the research or clinical purpose. Moreover, the disadvantages of one approach are often counterbalanced by of the other. The vast majority of clinicians view depression as a psychiatric disorder. This view is appropriate because knowledge about effective treatments for depression is largely restricted to clinical trials conducted with patients who meet the diagnostic criteria for depressive disorders. As noted below, however, some clinicians also worry that the criteria for depressive disorders ignore less severe but clinically relevant depressive syndromes.

Both conceptual orientations are relevant to research on the distribution and course and outcome of depression and the risk factors for it. Symptom scales have two major advantages over diagnostic measures. First and most important, symptom scales capture the entire range of depressive symptomatology, thus providing more information than dichotomous diagnostic measures. Research evidence suggests that this is important in that depressive symptoms that do not meet the criteria for a diagnosis of depressive disorder nonetheless often impair functioning, interfere with social roles, and compromise life quality (e.g., Berkman et al., 1986; Broadhead et al., 1990; Mirowsky and Ross, 1989). Second, because symptom scales are measured in a continuous metric, a broader range of statistical techniques can be used.

Symptom scales also have disadvantages. Most important, several relevant constituencies do not find symptom data useful. Clinicians need to know diagnoses to develop individualized treatment plans. Third-party payers are strongly resistant to subsidizing mental healthcare in the absence of a severe and disabling psychiatric disorder. Faced with scarce resources, policy makers understandably wish to target services to the most severely ill. Beyond these practical issues, because severely depressed persons are rare in community populations, they are often "lost" or diluted in studies based on symptom data.

The relative advantages and disadvantages of diagnostic measures are the opposite of those for symptom scales. On the positive side, diagnostic measures typically have been validated against psychiatrists' diagnoses and are, therefore, meaningful to clinicians, policy makers, and third-party payers. In addition, use of diagnostic measures inherently focuses attention on persons with the most severe and disabling symptoms. On the negative side, diagnostic tools ignore mild symptomatology (which is often sufficient to impair functioning) and generate dichotomous measures that are limited in terms of applicable statistical techniques.

DISTINCTIVE FEATURES OF LATE-LIFE DEPRESSION

Two distinctive features of late-life depression are directly related to how depression is defined, conceptualized, and measured. The first concerns the prevalence of depression in later life. The second focuses on relationships between conventional risk factors and depression during later life.

Age has a complex association with depression. For all adults, many more individuals report depressive symptoms than qualify for a diagnosis of depressive disorder. This discrepancy is especially large for older adults, however. In brief, older adults report as many depressive symptoms, on average, as their younger peers (e.g., Gurland et al., 1980; Blazer and Williams, 1980) but are less likely than their younger counterparts to receive a diagnosis of depressive disorder. The recent Epidemiologic Catchment Area (ECA) studies report especially low prevalences of major depression among community-dwelling adults age 65 and older. In four ECA sites, the six-month prevalences of major depression for persons age 65 and older ranged from 0.5 percent to 0.95 percent, whereas the prevalences for persons aged 64 and younger ranged from 1.5 percent to 3.1 percent (George et al., 1988).

There are several reasons that older adults may report relatively high numbers of depressive symptoms but be less likely than younger adults to meet the criteria for a diagnosis of depressive disorder. First, older adults may be more prone to mild depression than younger adults. Second, high rates of physical illness among older adults may lead to higher reports of depressive symptoms. Such symptoms may be less likely to affect rates of disorder because clinicians discount symptoms due to physical illness and because diagnostic tools also exclude symptoms that are likely to be due to physical health problems. Third, some clinicians and investigators fear that the diagnostic criteria for depressive disorder are not "age-fair." That is, older adults may present significant depressive syndromes that do not fit DSM-III and DSM-III-R diagnostic guidelines. For example, Blazer, Hughes, and George (1987) assessed 1,300 community-dwelling older adults, 27 percent of whom exhibited significant depressive symptoms. Only 0.8 percent of the sample qualified for a diagnosis of major depression, and 19 percent had relatively mild symptoms. The rest of the respondents appeared to be severely depressed but did not qualify for a DSM-III diagnosis. These data suggest that conventional diagnostic criteria may miss important depressive syndromes. This logic also may apply to other variables. Some observers, for example, question whether DSM-III and DSM-III-R criteria are fair to racial and ethnic minorities.

Several social factors are robustly related to risk of depression. Examples of such factors include demographic variables (e.g., sex, education, financial resources), chronic and acute stressors (including physical illness), and social support, which refers to the availability of friends and relatives who are willing and able to provide instrumental and affective assistance (for reviews, see George, 1989a, b). Whereas stress increases the risk of depression, social support can buffer the effects of stress, reducing the likelihood of depression. Paradoxically, many risk factors are more prevalent in later life than at younger ages (George, 1992).

Evidence to explain these paradoxical findings is unavailable, but two possible reasons come to mind. First, risk factors may be differentially salient at different life stages, and some of the important risk factors for a late-life depression may not have been identified yet. Second, if the diagnostic criteria for depressive disorder are not age-fair, relationships between risk factors and major depression may be diluted and missed. This explanation has limited and indirect empirical support: The relationships between depressive symptoms and conventional risk factors are stronger than those between depressive disorders and those same risk factors (e.g., Landerman et al., 1989). There are parallel findings when examining racial and ethnic differences in depression. Although racial and ethnic minorities are more disadvantaged than whites on standard risk factors, depressive disorders are no more prevalent among racial and ethnic minorities than among whites (Anthony and Aboraya, 1992).

FINAL THOUGHTS AND FUTURE DIRECTIONS

Conceptual frameworks are consequential. They determine what we pay attention to as well as what we disregard. They are used for important purposes. In the mental health field, they guide diagnosis, treatment, and decisions by policy makers and third-party payers. Ultimately, however, conceptual frameworks are tools—and like other tools, their worth is a function of how useful they are. Currently, there are two major conceptual models for understanding depression: the diagnostic model, and the continuum of symptoms model. Although some clinicians and investigators believe that one model is right and the other is wrong (with proponents for both models), I have argued that both are useful, in part because they have counterbalancing strengths and weaknesses. In addition, some of the most intriguing unresolved issues concerning depression in late life have emerged as a result of the use of these competing models.

Although much has been learned about depression in late life, additional research is needed. Two important areas for future effort were noted previously: (1) determination of whether the diagnostic criteria for depressive disorders are age-fair, and (2) understanding of why risk factors that are robustly associated with depression earlier in life are less powerful during later life. Another important area that is already receiving some attention is variously called "subclinical depression," "mild depression," and "minor depression" (for convenience, I will use the last term). Research on adults of all ages suggests that (1) the prevalence of minor depression (i.e., significant depressive symptoms, but failure to meet the diagnostic criteria for major depression) is substantially higher than that for depressive disorders, and (2) minor depression is associated with high use of health services, moderate functional impairment, high rates of absenteeism from work, and perceptions of poor life quality (Broadhead et al., 1990; Snaith, 1987).

Several questions about minor depression are high priorities for future research. Is minor depression a distinct psychiatric syndrome— or is it a precursor to full-blown depressive disorder? What are the course and outcome of minor depression—and to what degree do they resemble the dynamics of depressive disorder? What are the primary risk factors for minor depression—and are they similar to those for major depression? Minor depression during later life merits separate inquiry. Given past research demonstrating that substantial numbers of older people who experience significant depressive symptoms do not qualify for a diagnosis of depressive disorder, minor depression may be especially relevant to the mental health and life quality of older adults.

Acknowledgments

Preparation of this work was supported by two grants from NIMH (MH43756 and MH40159).

References

American Psychiatric Association, 1980. *Diagnostic and Statistical Manual of Mental Disorders, 3rd ed.* Washington, DC: APA.

American Psychiatric Association, 1987. *Diagnostic and Statistical Manual of Mental Disorders, 3rd ed.*, rev. Washington, DC: APA.

Anthony, J.C. and Aboraya, A., 1992. "The Epidemiology of Selected Mental Disorders in Later Life." In J.E. Birren, R. B. Sloane and G. D. Cohen, eds., *Handbook of Mental Health and Aging, 2nd ed.* San Diego, CA: Academic Press.

Berkman, L. F. et al., 1986. "Depressive Symptoms in Relation to Physical Health and Functioning in the Elderly." *American Journal of Epidemiology* 124(2): 372–88.

Blazer, D. and Williams, C. D., 1980. "Epidemiology of Dysphoria and Depression in an Elderly Population." *American Journal of Psychiatry* 137(4): 439–44.

Blazer, D. G., Hughes, D. C. and George, L. K., 1987. "The Epidemiology of Depression in an Elderly Community Population." *Gerontologist* 27(2): 281–87.

Broadhead, W. E. et al., 1990. "Depression, Disability Days, and Days Lost from Work in a Prospective Epidemiologic Survey." *Journal of the American Medical Association* 264(19): 2525–28.

Eaton, W. W. and Kessler, L. G., 1981. "Rates of Symptoms of a Depression in a National Sample." *American Journal of Epidemiology* 114(4): 528–38.

George, L. K., 1989a. "Social-Economic Factors." In E. W. Busse and D. G. Blazer, eds., *Geriatric Psychiatry.* Washington, DC: American Psychiatric Press.

George, L. K., 1989b. "Stress, Social Support, and Depression Over the Life Cycle." In K. S. Markides and C. L. Cooper, eds., *Aging, Stress, and Health.* Chichester, UK: John Wiley.

George, L. K., 1992. "Social Factors and the Onset and Outcome of Depression." In K. W. Schaie, J. S. House and D. G. Blazer, eds., *Aging, Health, Behaviors, and Health Outcomes.* Hillsdale, NJ: Lawrence Erlbaum Associates.

George, L. K. et al., 1988. "Psychiatric Disorders and Mental Health Service Use in Later Life: Evidence from the Epidemiologic Catchment Area Program." In J. Brody and G. L. Maddox, eds., *Epidemiology and Aging.* New York: Springer Publishing Company.

George, L. K. et al., 1989. "Internal Consistency of DSM-III Diagnoses." In L. N. Robins and J. E. Barrett, eds., *The Validity of Psychiatric Diagnosis.* New York: Raven Press.

Gurland, B. J. et al., 1980. "The Epidemiology of Depression and Dementia in the Elderly: The Use of Multiple Indicators of These Conditions." In J. O. Cole and J. E. Barrett, eds., *Psychopathology of the Aged*. New York: Raven Press.

Landerman, R. et al., 1989. "Alternative Models of the Stress Buffering Hypothesis." *American Journal of Community Psychology* 17(6): 625–42.

Mirowsky, J. and Ross, C. E., 1989. *Social Causes of Psychological Distress*. New York: Aldine de Gruyter.

Radloff, L. S., 1977. "The CES-D Scale: A Self-Report Depression Scale for Research in the General Population." *Journal of Applied Psychological Measurement* 1(3): 385–94.

Snaith, R. P., 1987. "The Concept of Mild Depression." *British Journal of Psychiatry* 150(2): 387–93.

Yesavage, J. A. et al., 1983. "Development and Validation of a Geriatric Depression Screening Scale: A Preliminary Report." *Journal of Psychiatric Research* 17(1): 37–49.

Anxiety Disorders in the Elderly

Bennett Gurian and Robert Goisman

nxiety may be defined as a subjective state of internal discomfort, dread, and foreboding, accompanied by autonomic nervous system arousal (Gurian and Miner, 1991).
Different from fear, anxiety tends to occur without apparent conscious stimulus. The term "anxiety" may refer to a mood state,
affect, symptom, disorder, or class of disorders. The physical symptoms
include hyperventilation, palpitations, sweating, diarrhea, trembling,
dizziness, headache, restlessness, and muscle aches (American
Psychiatric Association [APA], 1987). Such symptoms are mediated by
the neurotransmitters norepinephrine and gamma-aminobutyric acid
and are related to the so-called "fight or flight" response (Benson,
1975). Certain cognitive changes are also associated with anxiety states;
for example, impaired attention, poor concentration, memory problems, and cognitions with anxiety-laden content (Gurian and Miner,
1991; Barlow, 1992).

The various schools of thought within the mental health field have
described the etiology and pathogenesis of anxiety in various ways.
Psychoanalysis has seen anxiety as having a symbolic function that varies
according to its origin—id, separation, castration, or superego anxiety,
for example (Nemiah, 1978; Goisman, 1983). Behavior therapy sees it
as an initially classically conditioned response to biological arousal or
trauma that is thereafter maintained by avoidance (Mowrer, 1960;

Goisman, 1983; Amick-McMullen, Kilpatrick and Veronen, 1989). Cognitive therapy regards anxiety-producing thoughts, whatever their origin, as both expressing preexisting anxiety and in themselves causing or increasing anxiety (Beck and Emery, 1985; Barlow, 1992).

Whatever the causation, accurate diagnosis for elderly patients is complicated by the similarity between the somatic manifestations of anxiety and the clinical symptoms of common geriatric medical problems. For example, struggling for breath may reflect underlying cardiopulmonary disease; palpitations may have a basis in arrhythmias; sweating may be related to hot flashes, trembling to Parkinsonism, dizziness to decreased cerebral perfusion, headache to temporal arteritis, and the like. Most elderly with anxiety disorders are never seen by psychiatrists, because if they seek treatment at all it is usually with their family physician, especially when there is somatization such as chest pain, headache, or dizziness. These patients may feel anxious about benign symptoms, which may then engender further anxiety of a more purely psychological nature. Conversely, many older persons falsely attribute symptoms of anxiety to aging per se and may therefore deny or underreport such symptoms, thus leading to needless suffering.

CLASSIFICATION

A brief review of the seven specific anxiety disorders listed in the third edition, revised, of the Diagnostic and Statistical Manual of Mental Disorders (DSM-III-R), published by the American Psychiatric Association, may be helpful at this point. *Panic disorder* includes one or more unexpected and unprovoked panic attacks. Either four such attacks have occurred in the past month, or else there is persistent fear of another attack. At least 4 out of 13 possible symptoms must be present, and at least 4 of the symptoms have developed within 10 minutes of the appearance of the first symptom. Panic may occur with or without *agoraphobia*, which is the fear that one cannot escape or might be cut off from help in certain places or situations; less commonly, agoraphobia can occur in the absence of panic attacks. *Social phobia* is a persistent fear of one or more situations in which one might incur humiliation (e.g., public speaking). *Simple phobias* are persistent fears of specific objects or situations (e.g., snakes, heights) other than the fear of having a panic attack or of social humiliation. In each of these phobic disorders, exposure to the external phobic stimulus usually leads to the anxiety response, so these situations are either avoided or else endured only with distress. There are three anxiety diagnoses not related to panic or phobias. *Obsessive-compulsive disorder* may present with recurrent and persistent ideas that are intrusive and senseless (obsessions) and/or with repetitive and purposeful behaviors performed in response to an obsession or according to certain idiosyncratic rules in an attempt to neutralize or suppress discomfort (compulsions). Both obsessions and compulsions cause distress and take up more than one hour daily or interfere with one's normal routine. *Post-traumatic stress disorder* is the re-experiencing of an unusually traumatic event in a recurrent and distressing fashion, often with avoidance of trauma-related stimuli, numbing of general responsiveness, sleep difficulties, hypervigilance, difficulty concentrating, or an exaggerated startle response. *Generalized anxiety disorder* is manifested by unrealistic worry about 2 or more life circumstances for at least 6 months and by 6 or more of a possible 18 symptoms of motor tension, autonomic hyperactivity, or hypervigilance.

EPIDEMIOLOGY

Data on the incidence and prevalence of formal DSM-III-R anxiety disorders in the elderly is relatively scarce (Barbee and McLaulin, 1990), and in fact rates of diagnosis of such disorders in the general population may exceed those published for the elderly (Myers et al., 1984). Simple phobias may be more likely than other anxiety disorders to have an onset after age 60 (Thyer et al., 1985), but some clinicians have found reactive or generalized anxiety to be more common than panic disorder or phobias in clinical practice (as compared to epidemiologic samples) (Barbee and McLaulin, 1990). A comprehensive review by Blazer et al. (1991), which included Epidemiologic Catchment Area Project data, concluded that simple phobia was the most common anxiety syndrome among the elderly, with DSM-III agoraphobia next, followed by generalized anxiety, and then by the other anxiety disorders.

Some elderly may experience an anxiety disorder for the first time in late life, while others will continue to suffer with a preexisting anxiety disorder. Anxiety disorders are in general the most common of all psy-

77

chiatric disorders measured in community-based studies (Myers et al., 1984), although data from the Epidemiologic Catchment Area study showed that both the current and lifetime prevalence of anxiety disorders decrease with age for both sexes (Myers et al., 1984).

In one large study of older people (N=2,051), physical health had the strongest linear relationship with anxiety for both men and women (Himmelfarb and Murrell, 1984). High anxiety was associated with several medical conditions common in late life. There was a low correlation between age and physical health, which reduced the likelihood that age alone mediated the health–anxiety relationship.

Traditionally, theory has held that anxiety in older persons may appear as a response to a compounding of losses, increasing dependency, loneliness and fear of isolation, declining vigor, diminished sensory and functional capacities, change in economic or social status, feelings of uselessness, possible awareness of one's cognitive impairment early in dementia, and the approach of dying and death. Although a connection between these factors and clinical anxiety disorders appears intuitively obvious, adequate studies have not yet been done to substantiate a causal relationship.

Death anxiety varies with the individual and subpopulation examined and does not exist as a general characteristic of all elderly (Wagner and Lorion, 1984). For example, elderly African Americans have more anxiety concerning death than do Caucasians, women more than men, married more than single people, uneducated persons more than those with more education, and poor people more than those who are well-off. Importantly, neither death anxiety nor anxiety in general correlated directly with age, suggesting that it may be more of an issue of the middle-aged or "young-old" person beginning to face age-related concerns. The "old-old" may be less prone to anxiety in general by dint of their more extensive history of stress-inoculating experiences—that is, they may have become accustomed or desensitized to it.

Gurian and Miner (1991) point out that anxiety may be "a very common symptom but an uncommon syndrome" (p. 31, italics in original). Given this, the clinician needs to be vigilant regarding other DSM-III-R diagnostic categories in which anxiety-related complaints may play a significant role. For example, sexual dysfunction is not uncommon in the elderly (Gurian and Miner, 1991) and may both reflect and engender anxiety. The reality-based life stresses of old age may cause anxiety-related adjustment disorders. Finally, somatization and hypochondriasis are often anxiety-related manifestations and may be frequently found in this population (Salzman, 1982).

DIFFERENTIAL DIAGNOSIS

Excluding dysfunctions of the central nervous system, the most important psychiatric differential diagnosis is between anxiety and depression, particularly of the agitated type (Alexopoulos, 1991). This is particularly significant in that benzodiazepines, a legitimate anti-anxiety treatment, may exacerbate depression. Other psychiatric diagnoses to be excluded include hypomania and psychosis.

Further confounding the issue of differential diagnosis is the overlap between anxiety and agitation. Cole (1991) has pointed out that while agitation would appear to be a behavioral manifestation of anxiety, this is not necessarily the case; agitation can also occur in late-life schizophrenia, mania, organic confusion or delirium, dementia, alcohol or drug withdrawal, or akathisia (an abnormal condition characterized by restlessness). Correct diagnosis here is of obvious importance—for example, schizophrenic agitation might require prescribing a neuroleptic drug, while agitation from akathisia might require discontinuing it.

Medical differential diagnosis may include illness of virtually any body system: hyperthyroidism, hypoglycemia, pheochromocytoma or other tumors, mitral valve prolapse, drug intoxication (e.g., from alcohol, caffeine, amphetamines), drug withdrawal (e.g., from alcohol, benzodiazepines), iatrogenic drug reactions (caused by drug interactions or too high a dose), asthma, chronic obstructive pulmonary disease, hypertension, epilepsy, Huntington's disease, and multiple sclerosis (Raj and Sheehan, 1988; Cohen, 1991; Shamoian, 1991).

A very slight advantage occurs with aging in that autonomic nervous system reactivity tends to decrease, potentially decreasing the intensity of some anxiety syndromes. Sleep patterns change in late life, sometimes as a reflection of anxiety but often becoming an additional cause of anxiety. Hearing losses may engender social phobia, while Meniere's disease, Parkinsonism, and other disorders that impair mobility may increase the likelihood of agoraphobia.

PHARMACOTHERAPY

Although the benzodiazepines are the most widely used anxiolytic agents in all age groups, there is little reliable research to support effective or safe use of these drugs by the elderly. Most prescribing practices have evolved from clinical experience that often does not rigorously attend to issues such as side effects, documentation of specific outcomes, or comparison with control groups using other medications or no medication. Based on the limited data available, these agents probably are effective for treatment of anxiety in the aged, but they have a prolonged effect and may be more toxic than is acceptable, even at therapeutic doses (Salzman, 1991). Because of this, short-half-life benzodiazepines are better for older persons, even though they tend to be more difficult to withdraw, are usually sedating, and may cause confusion and other aspects of cognitive impairment (Salzman, 1989; Pomera et al., 1991).

The serotonin agonist, buspirone, is probably therapeutically equivalent to the benzodiazepines and is supposed to have fewer side effects. However, it has not yet been adequately studied in the elderly.

Beta-blockers may be of use in decreasing disruptive behaviors in elderly with dementia or other medical or psychiatric disorders, but there are few data to suggest their use in anxiety syndromes (Salzman, 1989).

Both cyclic antidepressants and monoamine oxidase inhibitors (MAOIs) have been used as anxiolytics, especially in panic disorder, again with little careful study in the older patient. Potential risks of anticholinergic and cardiotoxic effects with the tricyclic antidepressants or of hypertensive crisis with the MAOIs often outweigh the possible therapeutic benefits. The serotonin re-uptake-inhibiting antidepressants like Prozac may offer a better risk/benefit ratio, but little controlled research is yet available with this age group.

PSYCHOTHERAPY

Anxiety as a symptom is often reduced as a function of the establishment of a therapeutic alliance. The interest, availability, predictability, accessibility, empathy, and understanding of the therapist go a long way in calming, supporting, and reassuring the anxious patient. Isolated anxiety disorders are not that common among elderly. Most of the time anxiety is part of a more complicated syndrome, often with depression and often with other medical conditions. Therefore, psychotherapy with an older anxious patient is rarely focused solely on anxiety, but must also address the multiple coexisting issues (see chapter 12).

It has always been tempting to look for ways in which elderly are different from younger patients and, therefore, to justify modifications in therapeutic goals or interventions. This may be a subtle form of ageism. The elderly psychiatric patient may be best served by the therapist who is prepared to offer any and every treatment modality and technique available to the field, with energy and an enthusiasm that communicates a reasonable sense of optimism. There will be situations that primarily call for insight-oriented work, some that are best addressed with a combined somatic and psychotherapeutic approach, and others that are effectively treated by such means as reminiscence, support, or environmental manipulation.

Patients of all ages show a wide range of psychological mindedness (insight, self-awareness, acknowledgment of unconscious drives and defenses), responsivity, capacity for insight and growth, and motivation for change. Psychotherapy with older people offers the same range of benefits for the patient, the same types of satisfactions for the therapist, and the same series of challenges to be met by both patient and therapist as is the case in general.

BEHAVIOR THERAPY

In addition to techniques of psychodynamic psychotherapy, the somewhat newer schools of behavior therapy and cognitive therapy have much to offer in the treatment of the anxious elderly, in part because, when compared to anxiolytic medication, these methods have essentially no side effects (McCarthy, Katz and Foa, 1991). Relaxation training methods can be used as a primary treatment modality or as an adjunct to other behavioral or nonbehavioral techniques (Benson, 1975; McCarthy, Katz and Foa, 1991). Formal exposure treatment may be limited in its usefulness because of the relatively low incidence of true obsessive-compulsive disorder and agoraphobia among the elderly, but evidence of its effectiveness in this population when indicated does exist (Carstensen, 1988). Behavioral-skills training and problem-solving techniques may address reality-based environmental problems common to the elderly and hence help reduce day-to-day anxiety as well (Morris and Morris, 1991).

The methods of cognitive therapy may be useful as well, as long as there is no extensive organic cognitive impairment (Teri and Gallagher-Thompson, 1991). This form of treatment has been more extensively researched among the depressed elderly than in those with anxiety (Thompson et al., 1986), but there is some evidence that specificity for anxiety versus depression may not be a critical determinant of outcome (McCarthy, Katz and Foa, 1991). Further, many of the characteristics of cognitive therapy such as concrete goal-setting, higher level of therapist activity, and awareness of external limitations may be those most conducive to efficacy of any form of psychotherapy with older people (Morris and Morris, 1991).

FUTURE CONSIDERATIONS

Because of the uncertainty as to whether current diagnostic criteria for anxiety disorders are appropriate for use with the elderly, researchers face the task of redefining terms based on new inquiry into etiology, epidemiology, clinical presentation, and therapeutic interventions. This will depend heavily on the development of new rating scales that quantify dysphoria (feeling unwell or unhappy), whether it stems from "pure" anxiety or other affective states. Clarification also depends on progress made in understanding the impact on clinical symptomology of underlying changes in neurochemistry and neurophysiology of the aging body—whether they are usual and age-related or examples of late-life pathology.

All forms of treatment lack well-controlled studies of efficacy in the aged population. The "perfect" anxiolytic agent has yet to be offered. There are not adequate numbers of well-trained clinicians to begin to provide the psychotherapy or behavioral therapies indicated. New methods of recruiting anxious elderly subjects, as well as nonanxious elderly controls, are needed for research studies.

A better understanding of anxiety and aging is one aspect of the rapidly increasing body of knowledge within geropsychiatry. As the field advances, so will our ability to help older people who suffer with the myriad forms of anxiety.

References

Alexopoulos, G. S., 1991. "Anxiety and Depression in the Elderly." In C. Salzman and B. D. Lebowitz, eds., *Anxiety in the Elderly*. New York: Springer Publishing Company.

American Psychiatric Association, 1987. *Diagnostic and Statistical Manual of Mental Disorders, 3rd. ed.*, revised. Washington, D.C.: APA.

Amick-McMullen, A., Kilpatrick, D. G. and Veronen, L. J., 1989. "Family Survivors of Homicide Victims: A Behavioral Analysis." *Behavior Therapist* 12(4): 75–79.

Barbee, J. G. and McLaulin, J. B., 1990. "Anxiety Disorders: Diagnosis and Pharmacotherapy in the Elderly." *Psychiatric Annals* 20(8): 439–45.

Barlow, D. H., 1992. "Cognitive-Behavioral Approaches to Panic Disorder and Social Phobia." *Bulletin of the Menninger Clinic* 56(2, suppl. A): A14–A28.

Beck, A. T. and Emery, G., 1985. *Anxiety Disorders and Phobias: A Cognitive Perspective*. New York: Basic Books.

Benson, H., 1975. *The Relaxation Response*. New York: Avon Books.

Blazer, D., George, L. K. and Hughes, D., 1991. "The Epidemiology of Anxiety Disorders: An Age Comparison." In C. Salzman and B. D. Lebowitz, eds., *Anxiety in the Elderly*. New York: Springer Publishing Company.

Carstensen, L. L., 1988. "The Emerging Field of Behavioral Gerontology." *Behavior Therapy* 19: 259–81.

Cohen, G. D., 1991. "Anxiety and General Medical Disorders." In C. Salzman and B. D. Lebowitz, eds., *Anxiety in the Elderly*. New York: Springer Publishing Company.

Cole, J. O., 1991. "Anxiety in the Elderly: Research Issues." In C. Salzman and B. D. Lebowitz, eds., *Anxiety in the Elderly*. New York: Springer Publishing Company.

Goisman, R. M., 1983. "Therapeutic Approaches to Phobia: A Comparison." *American Journal of Psychotherapy* 37: 227–34.

Gurian, B. S. and Miner, J. H., 1991. "Clinical Presentation of Anxiety in the Elderly." In C. Salzman and B. D. Lebowitz, eds., *Anxiety in the Elderly*. New York: Springer Publishing Company.

Himmelfarb, S. and Murrell, S. A., 1984. "Prevalence and correlates of anxiety symptoms in older adults." *Journal of Psychology* 116: 159–67.

McCarthy, P. R., Katz, I. R. and Foa, E. B., 1991. "Cognitive-Behavioral Treatment of Anxiety in the Elderly: A Proposed Model." In C. Salzman and B. D. Lebowitz, eds., *Anxiety in the Elderly*. New York: Springer Publishing Company.

Morris, R. G. and Morris, L. W., 1991. "Cognitive and Behavioral Approaches with the Depressed Elderly." *International Journal of Geriatric Psychiatry* 6: 407–13.

Mowrer, O. H., 1960. *Learning Theory and Behavior*. New York: Wiley.

Myers, J. K. et al., 1984. "Six-Month Prevalence of Psychiatric Disorders in Three Communities." *Archives of General Psychiatry* 41: 959–67.

Nemiah, J. C., 1978. "Psychoneurotic Disorders." In A. M. Nicholi, ed., *The Harvard Guide to Modern Psychiatry*. Cambridge, MA: Belknap Press.

Pomera, N. et al., 1991. "Cognitive Toxicity and Benzodiazepines in the Elderly." In C. Salzman and B. Lebowitz, eds., *Anxiety in the Elderly*. New York: Springer Publishing Company.

Raj, A. B. and Sheehan, D. V., 1988. "Medical Evaluation of the Anxious Patient." *Psychiatric Annals* 18(3): 176–81.

Salzman, C., 1982. "A Primer on Geriatric Psychopharmacology." *American Journal of Psychiatry* 139: 67–74.

Salzman, C., 1989. "Improvement in Cognitive Function in Elderly Nursing Home Residents When Benzodiazepines are Withdrawn." Unpublished data.

Shamoian, C. A., 1991. "What is Anxiety in the Elderly?" In C. Salzman and B. D. Lebowitz, eds., *Anxiety in the Elderly*. New York: Springer Publishing Company.

Teri, L. and Gallagher-Thompson, D., 1991. "Cognitive-Behavioral Interventions for Treatment of Depression in Alzheimer's Patients." *Gerontologist* 31(3): 413–16.

Thompson, L. W. et al., 1986. "Cognitive Therapy with Older Adults." In T. Brink, ed., *Clinical Gerontology*. New York: Haworth.

Thyer, B. A. et al., 1985. "Age of Onset of DSM-III Anxiety Disorders." *Comprehensive Psychiatry* 26: 113–22.

Wagner, K. D. and Lorion, R. P., 1984. "Correlates of Death Anxiety in Elderly Persons." *Journal of Clinical Psychology* 40: 1235–41.

Mental Health and Successful Adaptation in Later Life

Edmund Sherman

he subject of mental health and successful adaptation in later life is one that requires a shift in perspective for most gerontologists. This is because much of our research has been conducted from what has been called the "misery perspective" on aging (Tornstam, 1992). That is, we have tended to study the "problems" of aging for the commendable purpose of correcting them through the development of new policies and practices. Although the intent is laudable, the result is that we tend to depict older people as more sick, feeble, and miserable than they really are. In order to say what is "successful" and "healthy," we have to be able to identify what is going well, not just what is going wrong, to identify those things "that enable humans to thrive, not merely survive" (Butler, Lewis and Sunderland, 1991). In Tornstam's words, we should "focus on such concepts as creativity, wisdom, and play."

Clearly, it would be mistaken to equate adaptation at the level of mere survival with mental "health." Yet, we know that failure of adaptation can lead to both physical and mental illness, so what is needed is a conception of adaptation that allows for a continuum of more or less effective adjustment to and interaction with the environment. Baltes and Baltes (1990) have found the concept of adaptivity to be very descriptive of successful aging. According to this concept, the criterion of success is "the efficacious functioning of the person in whatever system of goals and environmental contexts seems important," and this appears to have particular applicability for adaptation in long-term-care institutions (Baltes, Wahl and Reichert, 1991). According to these authors, the notion of adaptivity enables us to identify what is successful without having to specify a particular normative content of success, such as the developmental goals of generativity or ego integrity. They also feel that it gives more weight in determining success to the objective indicators of life conditions rather than subjective criteria such as life satisfaction.

The notion of adaptivity does, indeed, seem to have a great descriptive and operational value for understanding adaptation to long-term-care institutions. However, it is much more geared toward objective, subject-external criteria than the subjective, emotional, and attitudinal level of adaptation that is such an important component in any conception of mental health. It also seems to be less descriptive of both success and health for the overwhelming majority of persons 65 and over who are not in institutions but in the community, which is the domain of practice and research of this author.

In contrast, a number of authors writing from a life-span developmental perspective have proposed that successful psychological adaptation in the later years is marked by an integration and deepening of the personality (Butler, Lewis and Sunderland, 1991; Erikson, Erikson and Kivnick, 1986; Ryff, 1982). Whereas childhood can be defined as the period requiring the gathering and enlarging of strength and experience, old age can be defined as the period of clarifying and deepening what has already been attained from experience and from adaptation across the life span.

Ryff (1982) proposed a developmental orientation to successful aging that looks for the higher, more differentiated growth processes that occur with aging rather than looking at essentially nondevelopmental dimensions such as life-satisfaction as criteria of success. She also proposed that the inward-turning ego functions, known as the process of interiority (Neugarten, 1969), represents a key personality issue in old age and that perhaps it is through such inward turning that the emotional integration described by Erikson and colleagues is achieved. Certainly, the integrative, depth metaphor appears to have more validity and descriptive power than an expansionist metaphor for the realities of successful adaptation in old age (Kenyon, Birren and Schroots, 1991).

POSITIVE MENTAL HEALTH

More than three decades ago, the Joint Commission on Mental Illness and Health attempted to define "positive" mental health—that is, mental health as more than just the absence of mental illness (Jahoda, 1958). The commission was attempting to define for the field of mental health what is being attempted here for aging, a concept of mental health that implies thriving rather than surviving.

The commission came up with several approaches to positive mental health, and the first three of these have particular relevance here. First, it was suggested that indicators of positive mental health should be sought in the attitudes of the individual toward his or her own self, since various distinctions in the manner of perceiving oneself can be regarded as demonstrating higher or lower degrees of health. Second, another group of criteria should identify the individual's style and degree of growth, development, or self-actualization as expressions of mental health. These criteria are not concerned with self-perception as was the first approach, but with what a person does with his or her self over a period of time. Third, it was proposed that emphasis be placed on a central synthesizing psychological function, which was called integration, that incorporates some of the criteria suggested in the first and second approaches.

Briefly, then, self-attitudes, growth or self-actualization, and integration are the three interrelated approaches to be used here for identifying positive mental health in old age. It is noteworthy that the first two have to do with the concept of self, and the third with integration of aspects of the self. Now it is likely that the second approach having to do with growth or self-actualization is the most open to question as a criterion of mental health in old age, but the approach here is to focus on thriving rather than surviving in later life. Also, it was probably no accident that the majority of the self-actualized persons Maslow (1962) found in his psychological research were over 60 years of age. However, it is important to note that the term *self-actualization* as it is used here is more in the nature of self-realization and more a matter of self-understanding in depth than it is an expansion or aggrandizement of self in the external world.

87

IDENTITY, INTEGRATION, AND THE SELF IN LATER LIFE

When assessing mental health in the elderly we are, of course, more likely to see those persons who identify themselves by such adjectives as capable, active, valuable, as displaying positive mental health than those who identify themselves as old, tired, obsolete, and so on. Clearly, positive self-perceptions and self-esteem enhance morale and mental health. However, there is a sense of self, an identity, that goes deeper and beyond the personally enhancing self-perceptions described above. This has to do with one's identification with and commitment to something larger than the personal self. Thus, the older person's intergenerational identification with family, nation, culture, and religious belief become important components of a sense of self in later life. For this reason we need to be very concerned with issues of racial, ethnic, and cultural identity and how they affect the mental health of our elderly.

There is also the sense of self that Erikson and colleagues called "ego identity." Although ego identity versus role confusion is considered an issue of adolescence, it surfaces again in late life with the confusion inherent in the loss of occupational, parental, and other meaningful roles (Erikson et al., 1986). The issue of identity in old age goes even beyond the psychosocial identity of adolescence because the elderly have to review and revise their identities to conform with the lives they have actually lived, which Erikson and colleagues call "existential identity." They put it this way: "Out of this interactive process of evaluation and modification emerges the personal system of values, beliefs, and characteristics that comes to exemplify each elder's existential identity—that is, what his or her unique existence is coming to mean" (p. 140). Thus, we can look for evidence of such a process of life review and integration because its products of existential identity and ego integrity are indicative of positive mental health, certainly indicative of development of self in depth.

REMINISCENCE, ADAPTATION, AND MENTAL HEALTH

Butler (1963) observed that there is a natural increase in the frequency of reminiscence as a function of a life review process among the elderly. My own practice and research in the use of reminiscence suggests that certain types, as well as frequency, of reminiscence are reflective of three broad categories of mental health/illness (Sherman, 1991). Further, we found a correspondence between these categories and three general types or patterns of reminiscence (Sherman and Peak, 1991).

The first type involves the use of reminiscence for pleasure, to lift spirits and enhance self-image. It is therefore consistent with the positive self-perception criterion of mental health mentioned earlier. Indeed, reminiscence for pleasure is significantly related to positive mood and is the type of reminiscence most frequently used (Sherman and Peak, 1991).

The second type has been called "existential/self-understanding" and involves the use of reminiscence to solve past troubles, to achieve better understanding of self, and to determine life's meaning. Only about a quarter of the older people questioned claimed to engage in each of its uses.

The third type of reminiscence is used to solve present problems and cope with losses, and the small group (about one in 10) that made predominant use of this type showed significantly lower mood scores (Sherman and Peak, 1991).

The findings of Walaskay, Whitbourne and Nehrke (1983–84) of research on ego integrity status among the elderly correspond well with our results concerning types of reminiscence and adjustment. They found that the integrity-achieving group, which employed the "existential/self-understanding" type of life review, evidenced the highest degree of adjustment in terms of ego integrity. It was not the largest group.

Interestingly, the largest group was called "foreclosed" because they seemed to bypass the existential/self-understanding life review and to foreclose any existential identity in Erikson and colleagues' sense of the term. These individuals avoided negative memories in their reminiscence in favor of the more pleasurable, image-enhancing type. Indeed, they displayed good mood and morale, though they naturally had lower ego integrity ratings than the first group.

By contrast, another group called the "dissonant" appeared to be in an active life-review process, coping with problems from the past, and consequently showing lower current mood and morale. The lowest group in terms of adjustment, however, was the "despairing" because they expressed regret, hopelessness, and a fear of death in line with Erikson and colleagues' definition of despair.

The truly despairing elderly are apt to engage in an intense, obsessive type of reminiscence that is marked by rumination and perseveration on specific negative content from the past. Indeed, geriatric clinicians have identified this type of reminiscence as pathological and indicative of the need for treatment (Butler, 1963; Lo Gerfo, 1980–81). Wong and Watt (1991) also found a significant association between obsessive reminiscence and unsuccessful aging among the elderly in institutions and in the community. In a gross sense, then, it is this small group that could be seen as displaying in their obsessive reminiscence evidence of mental illness and unsuccessful adaptation, whereas the pleasurable image-enhancing and existential/self-understanding types of reminiscence seem to be associated with mental health. However, it is the existential, integrative type of reminiscence that is most associated with *positive* mental health according to the criteria proposed earlier. Wong and Watt (1991) found a significant positive association between integrative reminiscence and successful aging among the elderly in institutions and the community.

Why should this be so? Perhaps it is because integrative reminiscence is not just for reconciliation of the past but also for self-understanding to determine core values, beliefs, and behaviors that can be authentic expressions of each person's unique self—for being and becoming—within the reduced (hence priceless) time left in life. Perhaps it is because integrative reminiscence follows Socrates' dictum to "know thyself" and to lead the examined life. In any case, the review, reconstruction, and integration of the self in later life can be a creative experience in its own right (and even has elements of play) that can lead to wisdom. However, even for those who foreclose on this process, there is still the pleasurable, image-enhancing type of reminiscence to maintain morale and mental health, as most elderly do.

References

Baltes, P. B. and Baltes, M. M., eds., 1990. *Successful Aging: Perspectives from the Behavioral Sciences.* New York: Cambridge University Press.

Baltes, M. M., Wahl, H.-W., and Reichert, M., 1991. "Successful Aging in Long-Term Care Institutions." In K. W. Schaie, ed., *Annual Review of Gerontology and Geriatrics, vol. II.* New York: Springer Publishing Company.

Butler, R. N., 1963. "The Life Review: An Interpretation of Reminiscence in the Aged." *Psychiatry* 26: 65–75.

Butler, R. N., Lewis, M. and Sunderland, T., 1991. *Aging and Mental Health: Positive Psychosocial and Biomedical Approaches.* New York: Merrill.

Erikson, E. H., Erikson, J. M. and Kivnick, H. Q., 1986. *Vital Involvement in Old Age.* New York: Norton.

Jahoda, M., 1958. *Current Concepts of Positive Mental Health.* New York: Basic Books.

Kenyon, G. M., Birren, J. E. and Schroots, J., eds.,1991. *Metaphors of Aging in Science and the Humanities.* New York: Springer Publishing Company.

Lo Gerfo, M., 1980–81. "Three Ways of Reminiscence in Theory and Practice." *International Journal of Aging and Human Development* 12: 39–48.

Maslow, A. H., 1962. *Toward a Psychology of Being.* Princeton, NJ: Van Nostrand.

Neugarten, B. L., 1969. "Continuities and Discontinuities of Psychological Issues into Adult Life." *Human Development* 12: 121–30.

Ryff, C. D., 1982. "Successful Aging: A Developmental Approach." *Gerontologist* 22(2): 209–14.

Sherman, E., 1991. *Reminiscence and the Self in Old Age.* New York: Springer Publishing Company.

Sherman, E. and Peak, T., 1991. "Patterns of Reminiscence and the Assessment of Late Life Adjustment." *Gerontological Social Work* 16(1/2): 59–74.

Tornstam, L., 1992. "The Quo Vadis of Gerontology: On the Scientific Paradigm of Gerontology." *Gerontologist* 32(3): 318–26.

Walaskay, M., Whitbourne, S. K. and Nehrke, M. F., 1983–84. *International Journal of Aging and Human Development* 81(1): 61–72.

Wong, T. P. and Watt, L. M., 1991. "What Types of Reminiscence Are Associated with Successful Aging?" *Psychology and Aging* 6(2): 272–79.

Comprehensive Assessment
Capturing Strengths, Not Just Weaknesses

Gene Cohen

...an old age that adds as it takes away...   —*William Carlos Williams*

he biography of William Carlos Williams is doubly instructive in contemplating comprehensive assessment of older adults. Both a physician and one of the greatest poets of the twentieth century, Williams suffered a stroke at the age of 67 and was subsequently hospitalized at the age of 69 for severe depression. He was forced to give up the practice of medicine but went on to write some of his greatest poetry, himself illustrating "an old age that adds as it takes away" (Foy, 1979; Mariani, 1982; Cohen, 1988). This is a theme contained in Greek mythology in the myth of Teiresias, who after being blinded received inner vision that fully matured in later life; it was Teiresias who revealed the plight of Oedipus (Tripp, 1974). The point is that comprehensive assessment of older adults should identify not just weaknesses, but also strengths—not just problems, but also potentials.

GOALS AND COMPONENTS OF COMPREHENSIVE ASSESSMENT

Much research has been done and much has been written on assessing the older person presenting with clinical problems. For example, the Report of the NIH (National Institutes of Health) Technology Assessment Conference on "Evaluating the Elderly Patient: The Case for Assessment Technology" points out that "systematic and comprehensive evaluation of the patient's functional capacities and incapacities, as well as his or her social support system, establishes a rational basis for the development of treatment plans geared to the patient's biomedical, psychological, and social needs" (U.S. Department of Health and Human Services, 1983; Rossman, 1983; Rubenstein and Wieland, 1990). Note the emphasis on "capacities" as well as incapacities. This emphasis is further elaborated in the "essential components of comprehensive assessment": "(1) physical functioning, (2) mental and emotional functioning, (3) family and social supports,(4)environmental characteristics, (5) the need for specific medical or rehabilitative therapies, and (6) the potential for productive or personally rewarding use of time" (U.S. Department of Health and Human Services, 1983). Again, note number (6), which addresses capacity through a focus on the productive (Kahn, 1983).

The mental health and aging literature per se similarly has important reviews of the goals and components of assessing older adults (Butler, Lewis and Sunderland, 1991; Smyer, Zarit and Qualls, 1990; Kemp and Mitchell, 1992; Bergener et al., 1992). Moreover, the diversity of geropsychiatric assessment instruments that are available is significant and growing (Raskin and Niederehe, 1988; Poon, 1986). "In geriatric mental health, any assessment is done for one or more of the following reasons: (1) to establish a diagnosis, (2) to determine the personal, social, and environmental dynamics that maintain, control, and influence behavior, (3) to establish a baseline measure from which to assess the effects of treatment or natural changes in a disorder, and (4) to assess the person's ability to look after himself or herself and to function in various environments" (Kemp and Mitchell, 1992).

THE SETTING FOR THE ASSESSMENT

Relevant to element (4) above, various environments—the setting where an evaluation is conducted—can be a critical factor in arriving at the best diagnostic impression and treatment plan (Cohen, 1992). The home visit, in particular, can be invaluable. Many assessments are requested to determine not only a diagnosis for treatment but a determination of whether an individual still has capacity to live independently in the community; to determine the latter capacity, an evaluation at the older person's place of residence can offer a higher level of confidence in the decision-making process.

The home visit also offers unique training opportunities in assessment. An interesting example is with history-taking skills. A useful learning exercise for clinicians in training is to have them interview a patient in the office or clinic setting. Trainees should be encouraged to get as complete a mental picture as they can as to what the older person's living conditions are like, and then to do a follow-up home visit on the same patient to see how accurate their perceptions were. Not infrequently, students are stunned with the discrepancies they discover. This is a good home visit–feedback technique that is quite helpful in honing the art of history taking (Cohen et al., 1980).

MEASURES OF SUCCESS

Apart from the conventional goals and components of assessment, it is also important to consider measures of success—not only for the patient, but for both the significant other and the practitioner as well. Without an adequate assessment of outcome measures for all involved, the therapeutic alliance with the patient could be jeopardized at a later point in time. Similarly, the morale or motivation of family caregivers and healthcare professionals could be jeopardized by unrealistic or misunderstood objectives. For example, a goal for a person with Alzheimer's disease should not be improvement, or even maintenance of function, but rather alleviating suffering and maximizing coping at a given point in time.

OPPORTUNITIES IN THE FACE OF TRAUMATIC TRANSITIONS OR LOSS

The importance of assessing capacity in the face of loss cannot be overemphasized. This is where one truly encounters the basis for the ancient Chinese proverb that in every crisis lies an opportunity. Indeed it could be argued that individuals, like systems, tend toward equilibrium—that change or loss in one area is responded to in a compensatory manner in another area. And there is no endpoint in the life cycle for this potential.

Consider the case of Grandma Moses (Kallir, 1989; Cohen, 1988). When she was 67 her husband died; in dealing with this psychosocial loss and transition, she took up embroidery. By age 75, her arthritis was making it too difficult to embroider with the level of skill she demanded of herself; she was, however, able to paint, and began only then to approach painting seriously. She painted with excellence up until her death at age 101.

Consider, too, the case of William Edmondson. Edmondson had been working as a janitor at the Women's Hospital in Nashville up until his early 60s. When he was 61, the hospital closed, and Edmondson lost his job. He said it was then that he received his inspiration "to carve," and turned to sculpture. Over the next several years his folk art attracted attention, including that of a photographer who sent a photograph of Edmondson's work to New York's Museum of Modern Art. His sculpture became the first solo exhibition of the work of a black artist at the museum; it was 1937 and Edmondson was 67 (Livingston and Beardsley, 1980).

The case of Bill Traylor, another African American folk artist, reminds one—as does the case of Grandma Moses—that the ability to draw upon hidden or underutilized strengths applies to the old-old as well. Traylor was born a slave on a plantation outside of Montgomery, Alabama, remaining there as a farmhand after emancipation until the age of 84. By then his wife had died and all of his children had gone, so he moved to Montgomery. There he worked in a shoe factory until disabled for that work by rheumatism (analogous to Grandma Moses's difficulty with embroidery). He began to receive some financial assistance, sleeping at night in the storage room of a funeral parlor, spending his days on the sidewalk in front of a pool hall. But in 1939, at the age of 85, Traylor suddenly began to draw, telling a Collier's reporter, "It just come to me" (Livingston and Beardsley, 1980). His work was exhibited twice in his lifetime, and his drawing of Serpent created at the age of 85 was selected as the cover image of the catalog for the celebrated exhibition, "Black Folk Art in America—1930–1980," at Washington, D.C.'s Corcoran Museum of Art in 1980.

BIOGRAPHY CAN BE AS IMPORTANT AS BIOLOGY

While advances in the biological and neuropsychiatric understanding of mental disorders have been moving very rapidly (Hales and Yudofsky, 1987), it is important not to lose perspective on the continuing high value of psychosocial and biographical data (Cohen, 1989). This applies even to dementing disorders, where neurobiological considerations have been receiving paramount attention. The following case history illustrates the importance of such data.

Mrs. C, an 80-year-old childless widow, was seen because of a recurrence of depression. She had a fair degree of insight into the genesis of her disorder, recognizing a relationship between dark moods and dreams of having been scapegoated for family difficulties by her father. From early childhood she stood out in many ways, from ice skating skills, to good looks, to excellent job performance. But her father never seemed to recognize her achievements—instead, finding minor faults to criticize. Nonetheless, she was proud of her interesting experiences and accomplishments and took much satisfaction in describing them to the therapist and in registering his positive reactions.

As a young woman, while living in Hollywood, she had competed for boyfriends with some of the early starlets of the silver screen. She and Mary Pickford got involved with the same man; Mrs. C lost in that competition. She eventually married and settled into a steady white-collar job. By the age of 65 she was a widow and felt she wanted a basic change in life. Always having been an outstanding driver, she took a job that she described as "chauffeur for rich ladies." Here, as in all her activities, she mustered up great energy and dedication. To protect these "fine women," she decided to clandestinely "pack a pistol." She continued this work for about five years before going into retirement again.

Then at age 75, experiencing some financial strain, she relied once more on her diverse skills and resourcefulness and turned to the game of poker with considerable success in another circle of "rich ladies." By age 80 she had returned to retired life, spending increasing time with a new boyfriend. But shortly thereafter she lost the intimacy and companionship of this very dear friend with his death. Feeling suddenly alone, she began to review her disappointments in life, instead of her many satisfying experiences. The depression that gradually developed eventually led her to seek mental health treatment. Her depression finally lifted several months later when she struck up a close relationship with another man. She giggled over her awareness of a general pattern she recognized in choosing close male companions; for the most part they were older men, and she wondered whether this reflected longstanding attempts to somehow resolve ambivalent feelings she still had for her father. Her most recent romance was to be no exception, as she began dating a 97-year-old man. With the continued remission of her depression, therapy was terminated.

Three years later the therapist received distressing news. Mrs. C had suffered a major stroke, leaving her severely demented, with cognitive impairment similar to that of an advanced stage of Alzheimer's disease. The therapist went to see her in the nursing home. When he arrived, he was stunned with what he witnessed. Rather than the enthusiastic responses she had always attracted, Mrs. C now seemed to be looked on as a source of irritation to some of the staff. Her intellectual dysfunction, agitation, and high level of disability had made her quite difficult to manage. The therapist was struck by the matter-of-factness with which staff passed by her with minimal visual contact—in such contrast to the attention she had commanded throughout life.

The double tragedy experienced by the patient in relation to her history and her identity became apparent. The first tragedy was more obvious—the distance, the break from her own history, from her own past, due to the marked memory impairment. The second less obvious tragedy was the distance she experienced from others due to their separation from her, because of their inability to know about the interesting history she could no longer convey. In this regard, everyone has a compound history, a two-faceted history—a history of oneself as he or she knows it and a history of oneself as others know it. Not to be known by others, to be in effect without a history by being unable to relate one's past, puts a person at a severe disadvantage in eliciting the understanding and empathy of others; a competitive edge of the human condition has been lost. This is the plight of many patients with dementia, with Alzheimer's disease. Mrs. C had lost much of the appeal ordinarily derived from others having known her and known about her life experiences. This presents an enormous challenge and opportunity in assessing the patient; the opportunity lies in the positive impact that can be effected through conveying the individual's personal and dynamic history, his or her clinical biography. The focus on strengths cannot only be on the present, but also on the past, allowing one's history to be permitted an encore appearance.

An attempt was then made to restore some of this competitive edge, this most interesting human phenomenon—one's history, one's biography. Scrapbooks, photos, newsclippings, and other personal items of memorabilia were gathered in the process of trying to dramatically portray a sense of Mrs. C's past to the staff. The impact was pronounced.

When the therapist returned the next week, there was considerably more verbal and nonverbal engagement between the staff and the patient. And as more time passed, it became apparent that in addition to the staff feeling more in touch with the patient because of their being more in touch with her personal history, fragments of disjointed thoughts she expressed were somewhat better understood because of the enlarged frame of reference in which they were heard. Though the magnitude of the dementia was not altered, the patient's agitation was reduced and her connection with others enhanced; quality of life improved.

Families can greatly assist in this aspect of the assessment process, in helping staff to better understand the patient by becoming more familiar with the individual's personal history. Audio or video cassettes can be put together to make the history even more accessible, a process that can be very gratifying to family members, and a process that can enhance the overall patient/family/staff alliance. Such cases illustrate how biography can be as important as biology in the approach to assessing and treating patients—even those who are cognitively impaired.

Old age "adds as it takes away." In treating loss, the therapist can foster recollection of past accomplishments and experiences and at the same time tap into latent capacities. Comprehensive assessment of the older patient is incomplete without the latter.

References

Bergener, M. et al., eds., 1992. *Aging and Mental Disorders: International Perspectives.* New York: Springer Publishing Company.

Butler, R. N., Lewis, M. and Sunderland, T., 1991. *Aging and Mental Health: Positive Psychosocial and Biomedical Approaches.* New York: Merrill.

Cohen, G. D., 1988. *The Brain in Human Aging.* New York: Springer Publishing Company.

Cohen, G. D., 1989. "Psychodynamic Perspectives in the Clinical Approach to Brain Disease in the Elderly." In D. K. Conn, A. Grek and J. Sadavoy, eds., *Psychiatric Consequences of Brain Disease in the Elderly.* New York: Plenum Press.

Cohen, G. D., 1992. "The Future of Mental Health and Aging." In J. E. Birren, R. B. Sloane and G. D. Cohen, eds., *Handbook of Aging and Mental Health, 2nd ed.* New York: Academic Press.

Cohen, G. D. et al., 1980. "Geriatric Psychiatry Training: A Brief Clinical Rotation." *American Journal of Psychiatry* 137 (3) : 297–300.

Foy, J. L., 1979. *Creative Psychiatry.* New York: Geigy Pharmaceuticals.

Hales, R. E. and Yudofsky, S. C., eds., 1987. *Textbook Of Neuropsychiatry.* Washington, DC: APA.

Kahn, R. L., 1983. "Productive Behavior: Assessment, Determinants, and Effects." *Journal of the American Geriatrics Society* 31 (12) : 750–57.

Kallir, J., 1989. *Grandma Moses: The Artist Behind the Myth.* Secaucus, NJ: Wellfleet Press.

Kemp, B. J. and Mitchell, J. M., 1992. "Functional Assessment in Geriatric Mental Health." In J. E. Birren, R. B. Sloane and G. D. Cohen, eds., *Handbook of Aging and Mental Health, 2nd ed.* New York: Academic Press.

Livingston, J. and Beardsley, J., 1980. *Black Folk Art in America* 1930–1980. Jackson, MS.: University Press of Mississippi.

Mariani, P., 1982. *William Carlos Williams.* New York: McGraw-Hill.

Poon, L. W., ed., 1986. *Handbook for Clinical Memory Assessment of Older Adults.* Washington, DC: APA.

Raskin, A. and Niederehe, G. N., 1988. "Assessment in Diagnosis and Treatment of Geropsychiatric Patients." *Psychopharmacology Bulletin* 24(4). Rockville, MD: NIMH.

Rossman, I., 1983. "Comprehensive Functional Assessment: A Commentary." *Journal of the American Geriatrics Society* 31(12): 763–65.

Rubenstein, L. Z. and Wieland, D., 1990. "Comprehensive Geriatric Assessment." *Annual Review of Gerontology and Geriatrics* 9: 145–92.

Smyer, M. A., Zarit, S. H. and Qualls, S. H., 1990. "Psychological Intervention with the Aging Individual." In J. E. Birren and K. Warner Schaie, eds., *Psychology of Aging.* New York: Academic Press.

Tripp, E., 1974. *The Meridian Handbook of Classical Mythology.* New York: Meridian.

U. S. Department of Health and Human Services, 1983. *Evaluating the Elderly Patient: The Case for Assessment Technology* (June 29 and 30). Bethesda, MD: NIA

Aging and Decision-Making Capacity

Michael A. Smyer

he purpose of this chapter is to consider a basic question: What are the important unexplored research and practice issues at the intersection of decision-making capacity, legal perspectives, and processes of aging? The answer to this question requires a circuitous route through several related domains. First, a framework for considering the intersection of population aging, individual aging, and legal issues of decision-making capacity will be outlined. Next, epidemiologic data will be considered briefly to depict patterns of physical and mental morbidity in later life. Once this context has been developed, illustrative data will be reviewed focusing on a salient substantive issue—medication decision-making by older adults. The chapter concludes with a consideration of potential topics for further consideration. The research agenda outlined will be necessarily brief but also, I hope, enticing. The selections will reflect the range of concerns that await important work.

This article is designed to be illustrative rather than an exhaustive review of the literature. Fortunately, fuller treatments of the intersection of aging and legal concerns are available (e.g., Eth and Leong, 1992; Kapp, 1992), as well as fuller consideration of specific topics, such as informed consent and the elderly (e.g., Altman, Parmelee and Smyer, in press).

IMPLICATIONS OF THE DEMOGRAPHIC DATA

In a report prepared for the American Bar Association, Anderer (1990) recently reviewed state statutes regarding competency in determining guardianship proceedings. His work is of particular interest because it focuses on a timely and emotionally charged topic—guardianship and the criteria for determining whether an individual is incapacitated, incompetent, or disabled—in other words, whether or not the individual has the decisional capacity to manage him- or herself. Anderer's report notes that the last two decades have seen a shift from an assumption that old age is equated with incompetence. While each state defines incapacity in its own way and there is great variability from one jurisdiction to another, three key components or elements appear in the statutes: (1) disorders or disabilities, (2) decision-making/communicating impairment, and (3) functional impairment. Thus, recent developments have replaced a specified age with functional criteria for elements contributing to decision-making incapacity. Anderer reviewed each state's approach to guardianship and reached the following conclusion: "Most states use only one or two components. All three components should be part of any sound legislative scheme" (p. 4).

These three elements provide a framework for reviewing data on the functioning of older adults. Population-based estimates are available on disorders and functional disability and will be reviewed in the next section, but comparable population-based data are missing in the domain of decision-making/communicating impairment. A recent publication by the American Bar Association (1991) outlined the key elements of decisional capacity, as defined by the President's Commission for the Study of Ethical Problems in Medicine and Biomedical and Behavioral Research (1982), as follows:

> Decisional capacity requires, to a greater or lesser degree: (1) possession of a set of values and goals, (2) the ability to communicate and to understand information, and (3) the ability to reason and to deliberate about one's choices.

These themes are clearly congruent with the work of Appelbaum and Grisso (1988; Grisso and Appelbaum, 1991) in forensic psychiatry. Moreover, it can be argued that disabilities or functional disorders may impair decisional capacity. For example, Kemp and Mitchell (1992) recently summarized the importance of functional assessment in geriatrics and also highlighted the interdependence of psychiatric problems and ADL (Activities of Daily Living) functioning:

> Psychiatric disorders can and do directly affect ADL performance. Depressive disorders, anxiety disorders, cognitive impairment, substance abuse, and psychotic disorders all are likely to cause ADL impairment. Depression may affect all ADLs; dementia affects the subtle aspects of ADL performance, such as forgetting social context and standards for eating or toileting. (p. 677)

Kemp and Mitchell also point out that psychiatric and physical disorders will adversely affect the performance of IADLs (Instrumental Activities of Daily Living)—functional abilities that allow the individual to remain in the community. Similarly, the higher levels of functioning (skilled performance and social roles) assume a complete integrity of functioning that will be impaired by physical or mental disorders.

Collopy (1988, 1990) has also highlighted the importance of ADL and IADL functioning in distinguishing between older adults' decisional autonomy and autonomy of execution. As he notes, the older adults' decisional autonomy may become compromised when her or his ability to carry out decisions declines. Thus, a critical challenge for clinicians and service providers is facilitating decisional autonomy, even when executional autonomy may be impaired, as reflected in ADL or IADL difficulties.

With this distinction in mind, Kemp and Mitchell's discussion is helpful, since decisional capacity is assumed to be an operative element of the individual's functioning from the ADLs through performance of social roles. Population data are not available regarding older adults' integrity of decisional capacity. However, the hierarchical view of functioning provides a context for considering epidemiological data on the physical and mental disorders of the elderly.

EPIDEMIOLOGIC PERSPECTIVES: PHYSICAL AND MENTAL DISORDERS IN LATER LIFE

From available data, a number of patterns of physical and mental morbidity in later life can be discerned.

Chronic Disorders and Functional Disability

Cassel and her colleagues (1992) recently summarized information on the leading self-reported conditions for noninstitutionalized elderly in 1990. While 85 percent of the elderly have one or more chronic conditions, these data do not depict the impact of such conditions on self-care capacity and everyday functioning. Once again, the ADL and IADL metrics are useful.

Cassel et al. provide a useful summary of several trends. First, the rate of disability increases with age. For example, while approximately 23 percent of those ages 65–74 have difficulties with ADLs, roughly 45 percent of those 85 and older have such difficulties. Second, there will be a considerable increase in the size of the "disabled" elderly population in the coming decades. For example, there will be a 31 percent increase in those experiencing difficulty with ADLs in the 20 years between 1990 and 2010, and a 31 percent increase in those with difficulties in IADLs during the same time period. Third, and not surprisingly, the oldest age group (85 and over) will witness the greatest increase in the number of disabled elderly over the next 20 years.

Finally, House and his colleagues (1992) remind us that socioeconomic status (SES) affects the experience of age, chronic disease, and functional disability. Using data from the National Health Interview Survey, they depict cross-sectional age differences in the number of chronic conditions and activity limitation status broken down by SES. Again, several elements are noteworthy: First is the now-familiar pattern of increasing disability with increasing age. Second, and more important, however, is the fact that this pattern is mediated by the individual's SES. For example, the two lower SES groups reflect in middle age (45–64) patterns of morbidity that are not seen in the higher SES groups until age 75 and above. Thus, social stratification must be included when considering patterns of age, morbidity, and disability.

Mental Disorders and Aging

The discussion of mental morbidity will be necessarily brief and illustrative. However, several recent works have provided extensive discussions of the relationship of mental illness and aging (e.g., Birren, Sloane and Cohen, 1992; Blazer,1990; Light and Lebowitz, 1991) as well as the influence of aging on the presentation and treatment of specific disorders such as anxiety (Salzman and Lebowitz, 1991), Alzheimer's disease (Light and Lebowitz, 1990), depression (George, in press), and schizophrenia (Miller and Cohen, 1987).

Rabins (1992) recently reviewed the epidemiological data regarding the prevalence of psychiatric disorders across adulthood. He noted that the Epidemiologic Catchment Area (ECA) study provides the best available comparative estimates of rates of disorders (Regier et al., 1988). When the prevalence of any DIS (Diagnostic Interview Schedule) disorder is considered, older adults (those 65 and above) have the lowest prevalence (12.3 percent) of any age group. When specific disorders are considered, older adults again have the lowest prevalence of mental disorders of any age group, with one exception. When cognitive impairment is considered, older adults have the highest prevalence. Finally, when the prevalence rates for older adults alone are considered, two disorders are of particular concern: anxiety disorders (5.5 percent prevalence) and severe cognitive impairment (4.9 percent), both of which may have a direct effect on older adults' decision-making capacity.

The prevalence rates of severe cognitive impairment may vary, depending upon the assessment approach used (Johansson and Zarit, 1991). Regier and his colleagues (1988) report a 4.9 percent prevalence rate for severe cognitive impairment among those 65 years of age and older. However, the prevalence rate among the oldest age groups followed a now-familiar pattern, increasing prevalence with increasing age: 2.9 percent for those 65–74; 6.8 percent for those 75–84; and 15.8 percent for those 85 and over.

Comorbidity

The patterns of physical and mental morbidity presented thus far depict single disorders or disabilities. However, comorbidity of physical and mental illness and disability is far more common among older adults than earlier in the life span (George et al., 1989; Lebowitz and Niederehe, 1992). Cohen (1990, 1992) has noted that the interaction between physical and mental health in the elderly can take a variety of forms: Physical problems can lead to mental disturbance; mental distress can exacerbate physical symptoms; the combination of coexisting physical and mental symptoms can lead to a worsened clinical status; and psychosocial factors can result in an inability to manage a physical health problem. The implication of this interaction is that the synergistic impact of physical and mental conditions must be assessed in order to plan effective services (Gatz and Smyer, 1992; Verbrugge, Lepkowski and Imanaka, 1989) and effectively assess older adults' decision-making capacity.

In summary, demographic and epidemiologic data depict an aging society, with substantial increases in the oldest old—those over age 85. In addition, a substantial increase in the number of functionally disabled elderly is forecast. The data on mental illness and age are less comprehensive—providing only a cross-sectional view of current age differences in mental disorders. The cross-sectional view, however, shows clearly that cognitive impairment (particularly among the oldest old) and anxiety disorders are of substantial concern, both because of their prevalence and because of their impact on decision-making by older adults. Finally, the diversity of the aging experience must be underscored. Diversity can arise from cohort differences, from social stratification and SES effects, from gender differences, and from the unique patterns of comorbidity that present differing challenges for each older person. In the next section, the relevance of issues of decision-making capacity will be explored for a salient problem of everyday living (medication self-management).

DECISION MAKING IN EVERYDAY LIFE: THE CASE OF DRUGS

Recently, a number of researchers have focused attention on "everyday cognition," the functioning that underlies older adults' capacity to remain independent in the community. Much of this work has centered on instrumental activities of daily living. As noted earlier, the IADLs are important from both a clinical perspective and a legal perspective.

For discussion purposes, I will present information on one IADL, medication self-management, which is a useful example because older adults are overrepresented among the users of prescription medicines and because pharmacotherapy is an important element in the treatment of major mental disorders of the elderly (Salzman and Nevis-Olesen, 1992).

Although the elderly constitute only 12 percent of the population, they use over 30 percent of the prescription drugs and over 40 percent of the nonprescription drugs dispensed (HHS Inspector General, 1989). Current estimates are that the elderly spend about $7.2 billion each year on over-the-counter and prescription drugs (Brown, 1987).

Willis (in press; Willis and Schaie, in press) has focused on everyday cognition, particularly the cognitive components underlying the IADLs like medication self-management. Willis and Diehl (1989), for example, assessed older adults' ability to comprehend different types of information from prescription labels: the timing, dosage, duration, and instructions from auxiliary labels. They found that the level of comprehension varied for the different types of information on the label, but 50 percent of the sample got the dosage information wrong!

The implications for service providers working with community-dwelling elderly are clear: To be effective, we may have to use different approaches to providing information in different ADL and IADL domains. Moreover, we must adapt different strategies to assure that older adults are engaged in decision-making to the best of their abilities.

In summary, recent work on everyday decision-making, particularly in the area of IADLs, underscores the importance of altering the format and the substance of information in order to improve older adults' participation in decision making.

CONCLUSIONS AND SUGGESTIONS FOR FUTURE WORK

Current legal perspectives on decision-making capacity are not well suited to an aging society (Anderer, 1990; Kapp, 1992). Moreover, our clinical approaches to fostering independence in self-care capacity and everyday decision-making are still in their infancy. Thus, there are many pressing issues that remain to be explored at the intersection of our population's aging, legal perspectives on decision-making capacity, and the individual's ability to continue to be involved in decision making. The following list of topics that warrant further study is necessarily illustrative rather than exhaustive. Each is related in one way or another to two basic questions: What are the effects of age—or a combination of age and mental or physical disability—on the basic processes of decision-making capacity (e.g., understanding information, thinking rationally about treatment)? And, what are the implications of these effects?

Measurement Studies

Hofland and David (1990) recently summarized a review of assessment procedures for long-term-care settings. Their conclusion seems apt for geriatric decision-making in both community and institutional settings: "Present procedures to assess decisional capacity are seriously flawed" (p. 92).

It will be important to establish measurement equivalence in samples of older adults, as Grisso and Appelbaum (e.g., 1991) have done with other samples. Recent work by Janofsky and his colleagues (Janofsky, McCarthy and Folstein, 1992) offers a good example. Their efforts focused on the development of a brief instrument for evaluating the competency of patients to give informed consent or to write advance directives for medical care at the end of life. This type of study needs to be replicated and extended to other special populations of older adults, as outlined below.

Descriptive Studies

As pointed out earlier, there are no large-scale studies of rates of decision-making impairment among the elderly. Thus, it may be important to establish base-line descriptive studies of the rates of decision-making capacity and impairment with several subgroup contrasts:

- *Young-old versus old-old.* As outlined earlier, there are significant differences in morbidity and rates of impairment between those under 85 and those above.
- *Clinical populations.* As noted earlier, several of the most prevalent mental disorders affecting older adults (e.g., anxiety disorders, depression, and cognitive impairment from a number of causes) affect several of the key elements of decision making as outlined by Appelbaum and Grisso (1988). The precise impact of these disorders on older adults' decision-making capacity has not been fully explored. To date, there are no descriptive studies depicting the functioning of patient populations (with distinctive patterns of morbidity and comorbidity) on standard measures of comprehension.
- *Early onset versus late onset.* Within geriatric psychiatric populations, a

distinction is often made between those who developed a mental illness and grew old (early onset) and those who grew old and developed a mental illness (late onset) (e.g., Meyers and Alexopoulos,1988; Pearlson et al., 1989). The question of whether these patterns of onset are associated with different patterns of decision-making impairment is of some interest, but thus far there are no data available on this issue.

• Individual versus family perspectives. Aging is an inherently interdependent process. Many of the difficult decisions facing older adults—issues of healthcare, advanced directives, and assessing one's own capacity to remain at home—often involve their family members as well. The proper role of family members in decision making with and for impaired elderly is an issue that has generated substantial discussion regarding legal options (e.g., Areen, 1987; Kapp, 1991; Liacos, 1989), the role of healthcare providers (e.g., Lo, Rouse and Dornbrand, 1990), and the ethical issues inherent in interdependence (e.g., Jecker, 1990; Nelson, 1992).

Although there have been simulations with family members and elderly patients using vignettes (e.g., Zweibel and Cassel, 1989), we still do not know much about the patterns of congruence and disagreement between impaired elderly and their relatives. Do they vary by age (young-old/old-old)? By diagnostic group? Do we find consensus within families (e.g., do all the adult children agree)? We need more information exploring the intersection of "intimacy and impairment," as Nelson (1992) has called it.

Intervention Studies

At the same time that descriptive, baseline studies are being pursued, we should also "test the limits" of decision-making capacity of impaired elderly. Work that is analogous to the efforts of Grisso and Appelbaum (varying format, substance, and target patient sample) is sorely needed within the older age groups.

Work by Tymchuk and his colleagues (1988) provides one example of the type of inquiry that should be undertaken. They varied format and risk of procedure in descriptions for older adults and found that the simplified and storybook formats were associated with greater comprehension, particularly in the high-risk procedures.

Time of Measurement

The work of Tymchuk and his colleagues is also helpful in highlighting another aspect of assessing decision-making capacity in older adults: The importance of retesting and of designing assessment procedures that can capture intraindividual constancy and change. Tymchuk and his colleagues retested their subjects one week after the initial vignette presentation. They found significant differences across formats. Again, the storybook and simplified formats were associated with greater recall.

This work illustrates the importance of assessing intra-individual stability and change over time. It would be helpful to extend a repeated-measures design to clinical populations with fluctuating levels of lucidity (aba, 1991). Thus far, no data are available to guide researchers or clinicians in choosing a method or a time period for capturing intraindividual variation in decision-making capacity.

In summary, this chapter has sought to highlight the important unexplored research and practice issues at the intersection of decision-making capacity, legal perspectives, and processes of aging. The demographic data make a compelling case that these issues will assume greater societal and personal importance in the coming decades. Emerging legal perspectives highlight the significance of impairment and functional disability in assessments of older adults' decision-making capacity. Epidemiological data on patterns of morbidity and comorbidity—particularly among the oldest-old—also reflect the growing importance of considering these issues. Everyday decision-making (as reflected in ADL and IADL domains) offers one arena of emerging concern.

Finally, the brief listing of potential research topics reflects the important opportunities that await scholars, practitioners, and policy makers. These issues have great societal relevance, as reflected in the demographic patterns. They will also have increasing personal relevance, as reflected in our own aging and that of our families.

Acknowledgments

This work was supported in part by a grant from the MacArthur Foundation Research Network on Mental Health and the Law. A more extensive version of this chapter was presented at a meeting of the

MacArthur Foundation Research Network on Mental Health and the Law, September 25, 1992, Cambridge, Mass. The author appreciates the helpful comments of Marshall Kapp on an earlier draft.

References

Altman, W. M., Parmelee, P. A. and Smyer, M. A., in press. "Autonomy, Competence and Informed Consent in Long Term Care: Legal and Psychological Perspectives." *Villanova Law Review.*

American Bar Association (ABA), 1991. *Patient Self-determination Act: State Law Guide.* Washington, DC: ABA Commission on Legal Problems of the Elderly.

Anderer, S. J., 1990. *Determining Competency in Guardianship Proceedings.* Washington, DC: American Bar Association.

Appelbaum, P. S. and Grisso, T., 1988. "Assessing Patients' Capacities to Consent to Treatment." *New England Journal of Medicine* 319: 1635–38.

Areen, J., 1987. "The Legal Status of Consent Obtained from Families of Adult Patients to Withhold or Withdraw Treatment." *Journal of the American Medical Association* 258 (2): 229–35.

Birren, J. B., Sloane, R. B. and Cohen, G. D., eds., 1992. *Handbook of Mental Health and Aging, 2nd ed.* San Diego, CA: Academic Press.

Blazer, D., 1990. *Emotional Problems in Later Life.* New York: Springer Publishing Company.

Brown, J., 1987. "Prescription Drug Costs for Older Americans." *AARP Issue Brief.* Washington, DC: AARP Public Policy Institute.

Cassel, C. K., Rudberg, M. A. and Olshansky, S. J., 1992. "The Price of Success: Health Care in an Aging Society." *Health Affairs* 11(2): 87–99.

Cohen, G. D., 1990. "Psychopathology and Mental Health in the Mature and Elderly Adult." In J. E. Birren and K. W. Schaie, eds., *Handbook of the Psychology of Aging, 3rd ed.* San Diego, CA.: Academic Press, pp. 359–71.

Cohen, G. D., 1992. "The Future of Mental Health and Aging." In J. E. Birren, R. B. Sloane and G. D. Cohen, eds., *Handbook of Mental Health and Aging, 2nd ed.* San Diego, CA: Academic Press, pp. 893–914.

Collopy, B. J., 1988. "Autonomy in Long Term Care: Some Crucial Distinctions." *Gerontologist* 28(suppl.): 10–17.

Collopy, B. J., 1990. "Ethical Dimensions of Autonomy in Long-Term Care."

Generations 14(suppl.): 9–12.

Eth, S. and Leong, G. B., 1992. "Forensic and Ethical Issues." In J. E. Birren, R. B. Sloane and G. D. Cohen, eds., *Handbook of Mental Health and Aging.* San Diego, Calif.: Academic Press, pp. 853–71.

Gatz, M. and Smyer, M. A., 1992. "The Mental Health System and Older Adults in the 1990s." *American Psychologist* 47 (6): 741–51.

George, L. K. et al., 1989. "Concurrent Morbidity Between Physical and Mental Illness." In L. L. Carstenson and J. Neale, eds., *Mechanisms of Psychosocial Influence on Physical Health, With Special Attention to the Elderly.* New York: Plenum.

George, L. K., in press. "Depressive Disorders and Symptoms in Later Life." *Generations* 17(1).

Grisso, T. and Appelbaum, P. S., 1991. "Mentally Ill and Nonmentally Ill Patients' Ability to Understand Informed Consent Disclosures for Medication: Preliminary Data." *Law and Human Behavior* 4(3): 667–79.

HHS Inspector General, U.S. Department of Health and Human Services, 1989. *Expenses Incurred by Medicare Beneficiaries for Prescription Drugs.* Washington, DC: Department of Health and Human Services.

Hofland, B. F. and David, D., 1990. "Autonomy and Long-Term-Care Practice: Conclusions and Next Steps." *Generations* 14 (suppl.): 91–94.

House, J. S. et al., 1992. "Social Stratification, Age, and Health." In K. W. Schaie, D. Blazer and J. House, eds., *Aging, Health Behaviors, and Health Outcomes.* Hillsdale, NJ: Lawrence Erlbaum Associates.

Janofsky, J. S., McCarthy, R. J. and Folstein, M. F., 1992. "The Hopkins Competency Assessment Test: A Brief Method for Evaluating Patients' Capacity to Give Informed Consent." *Hospital and Community Psychiatry* 43: 132–36.

Jecker, N. S., 1990. "The Role of Intimate Others in Medical Decision Making." *Gerontologist* 30(1): 65–71.

Johansson, B. and Zarit, S. H., 1991. "Dementia and Cognitive Impairment in the Oldest Old: A Comparison of Two Rating Methods." *International Psychogeriatrics* 3(1): 29–38.

Kapp, M. B., 1991. "Health Care Decision Making by the Elderly: I Get by with a Little Help from My Family." *Gerontologist* 31(5): 619–23.

Kapp, M. B., 1992. *Geriatrics and the Law, 2nd ed.* New York: Springer Publishing Company.

Kemp, B. J. and Mitchell, J. M., 1992. "Functional Assessment in Geriatric Mental Health." In J. E. Birren, R. B. Sloane and G. D. Cohen, eds., *Handbook of Mental Health and Aging*. San Diego, CA: Academic Press, pp. 671–97.

Lebowitz, B. D. and Niederehe, G., 1992. "Concepts and Issues in Mental Health and Aging." In J. E. Birren, R. B. Sloane and G. D. Cohen, eds., *Handbook of Mental Health and Aging, 2nd ed.* San Diego, CA: Academic Press, pp. 3–26.

Liacos, P. J., 1989. "Is 'Substituted Judgment' a Valid Legal Concept?" *Issues in Law and Medicine* 5(2): 215–24.

Light, E. and Lebowitz, B. D., eds., 1990. *Alzheimer's Disease Treatment and Family Stress.* New York: Hemisphere.

Light, E. and Lebowitz, B. D., eds., 1991. *The Elderly with Chronic Mental Illness.* New York: Springer Publishing Company.

Lo, B., Rouse, F. and Dornbrand, L., 1990. "Family Decision Making on Trial: Who Decides for Incompetent Patients?" *New England Journal of Medicine* 322(17): 1228–32.

Meyers, B. S. and Alexopoulos, G., 1988. "Age of Onset and Studies of Late Life Depression." *International Journal of Geriatric Psychiatry* 3: 219–28.

Miller, N. E. and Cohen, G. D., eds., 1987. *Schizophrenia and Aging.* New York: Guilford Press.

Nelson, J. L., 1992. "Taking Families Seriously." *Hastings Center Report* 22(4): 6–12.

Pearlson, G. D. et al., 1989. "A Chart Review Study of Late-Onset and Early-Onset Schizophrenia." *American Journal of Psychiatry.* 146: 1568–74.

President's Commission for the Study of Ethical Problems in Medicine and Biomedical and Behavioral Research, 1982. *Making Health Care Decisions.*

Rabins, P. V., 1992. "Prevention of Mental Disorder in the Elderly: Current Perspectives and Future Prospects." *Journal of the American Geriatrics Society* 40: 727–33.

Regier, D. A. et al., 1988. "One-Month Prevalence of Mental Disorders in the United States." *Archives of General Psychiatry* 45: 977–86.

Salzman, C. and Lebowitz, B. D., 1991. *Anxiety in the Elderly.* New York: Springer Publishing Company.

Salzman, C. and Nevis-Olesen, J., 1992. "Psychopharmacologic Treatment." In J. E. Birren, R. B. Sloane and G. D. Cohen, eds., *Handbook of Mental*

Health and Aging, 2nd ed. San Diego, CA: Academic Press, pp. 721–26.

Tymchuk, A. J. et al., 1988. "Medical Decision-Making Among Elderly People in Long-term Care." *Gerontologist* 28(suppl.): 59–63.

Verbrugge, L. M., Lepkowski, J. M. and Imanaka, Y., 1989. "Comorbidity and Its Impact on Disability." *Milbank Memorial Fund Quarterly* 67:450–84.

Willis, S. L., 1991. "Cognition and Everyday Competence." In K. W. Schaie, ed., *Annual Review of Gerontology and Geriatrics* 11: 80–109. New York: Springer Publishing Company, pp. 80–109.

Willis, S. L. and Diehl, M., 1989. "The Elderly's Comprehension of Information Regarding Commonly Prescribed Drugs." Paper presented as a part of a symposium, "Facilitating Medication Compliance in the Elderly," 97th Annual Convention of the American Psychological Association, New Orleans, LA, August 11–15.

Willis, S. L. and Schaie, K. W., in press. "Everyday Cognition: Taxonomic and Methodological Considerations." In J. M. Puckett and H. W. Reese, eds., *Life-span Developmental Psychology: Mechanisms of Everyday Cognition.* Hillsdale, NJ: Laurence Erlbaum Associates.

Zweibel, N. R. and Cassell, C. K., 1989. "Treatment Choices at the End of Life: A Comparison of Decisions by Older Patients and Their Physician-Selected Proxies." *Gerontologist* 29(5): 615–21.

CHAPTER ELEVEN

Pharmacotherapy With Psychoactive Medications in the Long-Term-Care Setting

Challenges, Management, and Future Directions

Mark Monane, Jerry H. Gurwitz, and Jerry Avorn

D rugs are an indispensable segment of medical care of older nursing home patients. The majority of these elderly residents have multiple comorbid conditions, and pharmacotherapy is often employed in the treatment of the wide variety of disorders. In the institutionalized setting, the average resident is prescribed over eight medications concurrently (Soldo and Manton, 1982; Avorn et al., 1989). Nonetheless, the enormous use of medications in this setting must be carefully evaluated. Concern about excessive drug prescribing in nursing homes led to 1974 federal legislation requiring pharmacists to conduct drug regimen reviews in skilled nursing facilities receiving Medicaid or Medicare reimbursement (*Federal Register,* 1974.)

Studies to date have confirmed the high use (30–70 percent) of psychoactive medications in the institutionalized elderly (Office of Long-term Care, 1976; Kalchthler, Coccaro and Lichtiger, 1977; Beers et al., 1988). Ray and colleagues (1980) studied therapy for 5,902 Medicaid patients and noted that psychoactive medications were prescribed twice as often for the nursing home group, in contrast to an age-matched ambulatory group. Often these medications are used for inappropriate clinical indications (Beardsley et al., 1989; Garrard et al., 1991). Ingman and colleagues (1975) noted that the use of psychoactive drugs was "more frequently prescribed for symptoms than for diagnoses, i.e., for pain, restlessness, rigidity, sleeplessness or agitation." Buck (1988) found that medications started in this patient population were continued indefinitely without a thorough re-evaluation of their risks and benefits in the ongoing clinical scenario. Can this magnitude of drug use be justified in the care of the institutionalized elderly? How can it be made more appropriate? What are the challenges facing the clinician in the use of pharmacotherapy in the long-term-care setting?

CHALLENGES

Lack of Consensus on Drug Prescribing

In a review of nursing home care, Rango (1982) noted that overuse of medications was "the most common error of commission." Nonetheless, defining what is appropriate medication use in the nursing home is not always straightforward (Gurwitz, Soumerai and Avorn, 1990). Using what is called the Delphi method for developing a consensus among experts, a group of investigators developed guidelines for medication use in the nursing home setting (Beers et al., 1991). A panel of nationally recognized experts were able to agree on several medications to be avoided in the nursing home setting, such as amitriptyline and long-acting benzodiazepines such as diazepam and flurazepam, as well as on dose considerations for haloperidol and thioridazine. However, the lack of consensus on such matters as indications for the use of haloperidol and thioridazine in the nonpsychotic patient and the use of diphenhydramine as a sedative-hypnotic agent is a concern. These areas of nonconsensus result from the absence of enough well-conducted and geriatrically relevant studies in these areas.

Pharmacokinetics and Pharmacodynamics

A rational approach to drug therapy in the elderly nursing home resident requires an understanding of the effects of age on response to drugs. Pharmacokinetic issues to be considered in the elderly patient include absorption, distribution, metabolism, and excretion (Avorn and Gurwitz, 1990). Absorption is generally unchanged in the elderly, despite changes in the aging gastrointestinal system (Schmucker, 1985). Changes in drug distribution, often given little attention in the elderly, are related to changes in body composition with aging, which include a decrease in lean muscle mass and an increase in fatty tissue (Buskirk, 1985). The liver is the major site for drug metabolism and is important in the process of drug clearance. Phase I metabolic reactions, such as oxidation, hydroxylation, and phosphorylation, are impaired with advancing age, while Phase II metabolic reactions such as conjugations are relatively spared. Excretion is impaired because of a loss of functioning nephrons (Rowe et al., 1976).

Such age-related pharmacokinetic changes affect the serum half-life, which is proportional to the volume of distribution and inversely proportional to the clearance of all medications. As noted above, the volume of distribution of many lipid-soluble medications is markedly increased in the elderly. In addition, agents metabolized through Phase I mechanisms as well as renally excreted medications will have a decreased clearance from the body. The result will be a particularly prolonged duration of action.

Pharmacodynamic issues include an increased sensitivity with age to many commonly used medications. The study of this phenomenon is complicated by the fact that reduced clearance of the drug also is noted in older people, resulting in higher serum levels; one must control for the concentration of the drug made available to the receptor. Impaired performance of patients given benzodiazepines has been noted at significantly lower serum levels in elderly versus young patients, and similar increased sensitivities have also been reported with opiate use (Bellville et al., 1971; Castleden et al., 1977; Reidenberg et al., 1978; Kaiko, 1980; Scott and Stanski, 1987).

Polypharmacy

As people age, they are increasingly likely to be taking more than one drug simultaneously, so polypharmacy "may be the curse of the geriatric patient" (Beber, 1978). One may speculate, however, that the appropriate use of multiple medications in the elderly is not per se clinically undesirable for patients with multiple diseases. Such use is known as polymedicine (Simonson, 1986). It is distinct from the following seven features that characterize inappropriate use of multiple medications: use of medications that have no apparent indication, use of duplicate medications, concurrent use of interacting medication, use of contraindicated medication, use of inappropriate dosages, use of drug therapy to treat adverse drug reactions, and improvement following discontinuation of medications (Simonson, 1984).

MANAGEMENT OF COMMON CLINICAL DISORDERS

A look at the management of common clinical disorders seen in the long-term-care setting underscores the importance of the principles as outlined above. Insomnia and dementia are two examples.

Insomnia

Nonpharmacologic approaches to insomnia, such as attention to sleep hygiene and environmental/physical strategies (see Table 11.1), should be attempted before prescribing a sedative-hypnotic or in conjunction with the use of pharmacologic therapy (Monane, 1992). When sleep disorders are severe and do not respond to these nonpharmacologic approaches, a number of medications are currently available for use. Intermediate-acting benzodiazepines such as lorazepam, oxazepam, and temazepam, with half-lives of 8 to 15 hours, are metabolized by phase II conjugation pathways that are generally unchanged in the elderly. In addition, these medications have few or no active metabolites. Because of these properties, use of these agents has been recommended for pharmacological intervention in the elderly. Triazolam, the shortest acting benzodiazepine with a half-life of 2 to 5 hours, has gained wide popularity since its introduction because of its short half-life and concomitant lack of accumulation in the body. However, this same characteristic makes it ineffective for treating the early morning insomnia often associated with aging. In addition, Greenblatt and colleagues (1991) found higher triazolam levels and lower triazolam clearance in an elderly versus younger cohort given single-dose therapy, and also observed profound decrements in learning in the elderly group after triazolam administration. While long-acting benzodiazepines such as flurazepam represented an important improvement over barbiturates when introduced in 1970, these highly lipid-soluble agents metabolized through phase I reactions are frequently associated with adverse central nervous system side effects such as confusion, ataxia, and daytime sedation as well as systemic side effects such as falls, particularly in higher doses (Greenblatt, Allen and Shader, 1977; Greenblatt et al.,

1981). Given the availability of intermediate-acting agents, long-acting benzodiazepines should also be avoided in the elderly.

Dementia

Approximately one-third of older patients in the nursing home setting have dementia (National Center for Health Statistics, 1976). Dementia and its consequences represent one of the most common reasons for institutionalization. Management of dementia, both nonpharmacologic and pharmacologic, takes on increased importance for healthcare providers in the nursing home, and appropriate guidelines should be followed (see Table 11.2). A careful medical history and physical examination may uncover a treatable cause of agitation. When considering whether to medicate a patient with a neuroleptic agent, the side-effect profiles of these medications must always be considered. For example, all of the classical signs and symptoms of Parkinson's disease can be mimicked by side effects of neuroleptic medication (Spira et al., 1984). Akathisia, an uncontrollable need to move around, change position, stand up, and pace, can also be the result of neuroleptic medication. However, it is often mistaken as a sign that the patient remains agitated, leading to the use of even more neuroleptic medication.

Table 11.1 Sleep Hygiene Techniques

1. Limit caffeinated beverages to the morning hours

2. Keep bedtimes regular and sensible

3. Avoid daytime napping

4. Engage in a program of regular exercise.

FUTURE DIRECTIONS

Several factors may mitigate against multiple drug use in the older population. Few currently available drugs have precise and specific mechanisms of action. For example, amitriptyline is useful in alleviating depression in the elderly but has anticholinergic and alpha-adrenergic properties that may aggravate diseases commonly found in this age group. Designer drugs of the future will focus on specific receptors and end-pathways to control illness rather than affecting multiple receptor types and processes throughout the body (Jack, 1989).

Greater emphasis on geriatrics education has already occurred in

Table 11.2 Antipsychotic Medication Guidelines

1. Before starting an antipsychotic drug, identify the specific-target behavior to be treated and define the goals of therapy.

2. Use the lowest possible doses.

3. Prescribe short courses of treatment.

4. Monitor closely for side effects in all patients receiving these drugs.

5. After the situation has stabilized, consider a plan of gradually withdrawing neuroleptic medication.

Table 11.3 Questions to Ask Before Prescribing Medication

1. Can I avoid using a drug here?

2. Could stopping a medicine help with the patient's symptoms?

3. Is this the lowest feasible dose?

4. Does this drug have any particular side effects that are more likely to occur in an elderly patient?

medical curricula, and even more emphasis is needed in the future. Robert Butler's call for action in 1981 did lead to increased affiliations between medical schools and nursing homes for teaching, research, and clinical care (Schneider, Ory and Aung., 1987). In an effort to improve the effectiveness and safety of psychoactive drug use in the nursing home setting, Avorn and his colleagues (1990, 1992) introduced a a university-based educational outreach program, sometimes referred to as "academic detailing," to physicians, nurses, and aides in six nursing homes; six other homes served as controls. The follow-up evaluation performed six months after the initial evaluation document-ed a marked decrease in antipsychotic and benzodiazepine use in experimental versus control homes, and no increase in disruptive behavior or staff distress was documented. A study by Gurwitz and his colleagues (1992) showed similar improved prescribing practices with histamine2-receptor antagonists. These studies demonstrate the effica-cy of educational interventions to promote therapeutically appropriate reductions in drug utilization in the long-term setting.

Whatever the major developments, some degree of progress will be made if clinicians will only ask the basic questions, presented here in Table 11.3, before making any pharmacotherapeutic decision regard-ing elderly nursing home residents.

Acknowledgments

This work was sponsored in part by the Merck/AFAR Fellowship in Geriatric Clinical Pharmacy (Dr. Monane), the Clinical Investigator Award of the National Institute on Aging (Dr. Gurwitz), and the Program on Medications and the Elderly of the John A. Hartford Foundation of New York City.

References

Avorn, J. and Gurwitz, J., 1990. "Principles of Pharmacology." In C. K. Cassel et al., eds., *Geriatric Medicine.* New York: Springer-Verlag.

Avorn, J. et al., 1989. "Use of Psychoactive Medication and the Quality of Care in Rest Homes." *New England Journal of Medicine* 320: 227–32.

Avorn, J. et al., 1992. "A Randomized Trial of a Program to Reduce the Use of Psychoactive Drugs in Nursing Homes." *New England Journal of Medicine* 327: 168–73.

Beardsley, R. S. et al., 1989. "Prescribing of Psychotropics in Elderly Nursing Home Patients." *Journal of the American Geriatrics Society* 37: 327–30.

Beber, C. R., 1978. "Risk of Susceptibility to Pharmacologic Iatrogenic Problems in the Elderly." In C. Beber and P. Lamy, eds., *Management and Education of the Elderly.* Washington, DC: Excerpta Medica, pp. 11–12.

Beers, M. et al., 1988. "Psychoactive Medication Use in Intermediate-Care Facility Residents." *Journal of the American Medical Association* 260: 3016–20.

Beers, M. H. et al., 1991. "Explicit Criteria for Determining Inappropriate Medication Use in Nursing Home Residents." *Archives of Internal Medicine* 151: 1825–32.

Bellville, J. W. et al., 1971. "Influence of Age on Pain Relief from Analgesics." *Journal of the American Medical Association* 217: 1835–41.

Buck, J. A., 1988. "Psychotropic Drug Practice in Nursing Homes." *Journal of the American Geriatrics Society* 36: 409–18.

Buskirk, E. R., 1985. "Health Maintenance and Longevity: Exercise." In C. Finch and E. Schneider, eds., *Handbook of the Biology of Aging, 2nd ed.* New York: Van Nostrand Reinhold, pp. 898–99.

Castleden, C. M. et al., 1977. "Increased Sensitivity to Nitrazepam in Old Age." *British Medical Journal* 1: 10–12.

Federal Register, 1974. "Conditions of participation—pharmaceutical services." 39: 12–17.

Garrard, J. et al., 1991. "Evaluation of Neuroleptic Drug Use by Nursing Home Elderly under Proposed Medicare and Medicaid Regulations." *Journal of the American Medical Association* 265: 463–67.

Greenblatt, D. J., Allen, M. D. and Shader, R. I., 1977. "Toxicity of High-Dose Flurazepam in the Elderly." *Clinical Pharmacology and Therapeutics* 21: 355–61.

Greenblatt, D. J. et al., 1981. "Kinetics and Clinical Effects of Flurazepam in Young and Elderly Noninsomniacs." *Clinical Pharmacology and Therapeutics* 30: 475–86.

Greenblatt, D. J. et al., 1991. "Sensitivity to Triazolam in the Elderly." *New England Journal of Medicine* 324: 1691–98.

Gurwitz, J. H., Soumerai, S. B. and Avorn, J., 1990. "Improving Medication Prescribing and Utilization in the Nursing Home." *Journal of the American Geriatrics Society* 38: 562–52.

Gurwitz, J. H., Noonan J. P. and Soumerai, S. B., 1992. "Reducing the Use of H2-Receptor Antagonists in the Long-Term-Care Setting." *Journal of the American Geriatrics Society* 40: 359–64.

Ingman, S. R. et al., 1975. "A Survey of the Prescribing and Administration of Drugs in a Long-term Care Institution for the Elderly." *Journal of the American Geriatrics Society* 23: 309–16.

Jack, D., 1989. "The Challenge of Drug Discovery." *Drug Design and Discovery* 4: 167-86.

Kaiko, R. F., 1980. "Age and Morphine Analgesia in Cancer Patients with Postoperative Pain." *Clinical Pharmacology and Therapeutics* 28: 823–26.

Kalchthler, T., Coccaro, E. and Lichtiger S., 1977. "Incidence of Polypharmacy in a Long-term Care Facility." *Journal of the American Geriatrics Society* 25: 308–13.

Monane, M., 1992. "Insomnia in the Elderly." *Journal of Clinical Psychiatry* 53(suppl): 23–28.

National Center for Health Statistics, 1976. *Characteristics of Nursing Home Residents, Health Status and Care Reviewed.* Vital and Health Statistics, Series 13.

Office of Long-Term Care, U.S. Department of Health, Education, and Welfare, 1976. *Physician's Drug Prescribing Patterns in Skilled Nursing Facilities,* Publication (OS)76–50050.

Rango, N., 1982. "Nursing Home Care in the United States: Prevailing Conditions and Policy Implications." *New England Journal of Medicine* 307: 883–89.

Ray, W. A., Federspiel, C. F. and Schaffner W., 1980. "A Study of Antipsychotic Drug Use in Nursing Homes: Epidemiological Evidence Suggesting Misuse."*American Journal of Public Health* 70: 485–91.

Reidenberg, M. M. et al., 1978. "Relationship Between Diazepam Dose, Plasma Level, Age, and Central Nervous System Depression." *Clinical Pharmacology and Therapeutics* 23: 371–74.

Rowe, J. W. et al., 1976. "The Effects of Age on Creatinine Clearance in Man." *Journal of Gerontology* 31: 155–63.

Schmucker, D. L., 1985. "Aging and Drug Disposition: An Update." *Pharmacological Reviews* 37: 133–48.

Schneider, E. L., Ory, M. and Aung, M. L., 1987. "Teaching Nursing Homes Revisited: Survey of Affiliations between American Medical Schools and Long-term Care Facilities." *Journal of the American Medical Association* 257: 2771–75.

Scott, J. C. and Stanski, D. R., 1987. "Decreased Fentanyl and Alfentanil Dose Requirements with Age: A Simultaneous Pharmacokinetics and Pharmacodynamic Evaluation." *Journal of Pharmacology and Experimental Therapeutics* 240: 159–66.

Simonson, W., 1984. *Medications and the Elderly: A Guide for Promoting Proper Use.* Rockville, MD: Aspen Systems Corporation.

Simonson, W., 1986. "The Viewpoint of a Clinical Pharmacist." *Gerontologist*

26: 599–603.

Soldo, B. J. and Manton, K. G., 1982. "Demography: Characteristics and Implications of an Aging Population." In J. W. Rowe and R. W. Besdine, eds., *Geriatric Medicine*. Boston: Little, Brown.

Soumerai, S. B. and Avorn, J., 1990. "Principles of Educational Outreach ('Academic Detailing') to Improve Clinical Decision Making." *Journal of the American Medical Association* 263: 549–56.

Spira N. et al., 1984. "Treatment of Agitation and Psychosis." In C. Salzman, ed., *Clinical Geriatric Psychopharmacology*. New York: McGraw-Hill.

Psychotherapy as Applied Gerontology

A Contextual, Cohort-Based Maturity-Specific Challenge Model

Bob G. Knight

sychotherapy with older adults has been done, discussed, and studied for about eight decades. In general, both the case studies and the controlled research on outcomes have been positive (Knight, Kelly and Gatz, 1992). For the most part, psychotherapists who have worked with older adults describe the experience as valuable for clients and rewarding for the therapist, whereas those who have not argue that the aged cannot benefit from psychotherapy. Since the 1970s, the literature on therapy with older adults has increasingly drawn upon scientific gerontology (Knight, Kelly and Gatz, 1992).

The early history of gerontology as a discipline was characterized by a split between researchers, who were discovering that aging is a more positive experience than society presumably believed, and practitioners, who were struggling with the problems of a select group of elderly and who generalized the real problems of frail older adults to all aging persons. The loss-deficit model of aging, which portrays the normative course of later life as a series of losses and the typical response as depression, has been an integral part of the practitioner heritage.

Recent discoveries tend to undermine that picture. Retirement and the empty nest phase of marriage have been found to be related to increases in life satisfaction for many older adults. Life satisfaction seems to be stable over the adult life span (Costa et al., 1987). The

NIMH Epidemiologic Catchment Area Studies found lower prevalence rates of depression and other mental disorder in older adults as compared to younger adults (Myers et al., 1984). Gatz and Hurwicz (1990), in a cross-sectional study with a large sample, failed to find higher rates of depression among older adults; in fact, depressed mood scores were higher for the youngest group.

As a clinician, I have often asked myself, "Why aren't older adults more depressed?" As a younger adult, I find that the problems of older clients seem more real and more overwhelming than those that upset my age mates (and me). Clients' problems must be evaluated within the context of their developmental level and the tasks facing them. However, after spending years discussing the death of loved ones and confrontation with chronic, progressive disease, it has become difficult for me to be empathetic with younger adults who are distraught because their parents disapprove of their choice of job or mate.

With the accumulation of clinical experience, I have come to appreciate the significant ways in which older adults are indeed more mature. Most immediately apparent in the psychotherapeutic relationship is the greater acceptance of the finitude of life and a greater comfort in talking about death. The accumulated observations of people and relationships also form the basis of a fairly well-developed implicit personality theory for many older people. To go further with the notion requires a return to theoretical and research gerontology. As outlined in Table 12.1, a contextual, cohort- based maturity-specific challenge model provides a useful framework for considering issues of psychotherapy with the elderly. Each element of the framework will be discussed briefly.

EVIDENCE OF INCREASING MATURITY THROUGH ADULTHOOD

In a now classic discussion of personality across the life span, Neugarten (1977) suggested that, with age, there is an increase in interiority, a tendency to turn inward and become more reflective, psychologically oriented, and philosophical about life. This change would, of course, make older adults more suited for psychotherapy.

Although fluid intelligence (e.g., perceiving patterns in novel stimuli and speed of processing) declines with age, crystal intelligence (e.g., knowledge, vocabulary) likely remains stable. Cognitive maturation throughout adulthood and into later life may also be characterized by the development of "expert systems," dependent on the individual's experiences in adult life, and of movement to a stage of postformal reasoning with an appreciation of the dialectical nature of argument and social change and a greater appreciation of the fact that people hold differing points of view (Rybash, Hoyer and Roodin, 1986).

On the emotional side, older adults have been seen as becoming less impulsive and driven by anxiety (Gynther, 1979) and more emotionally complex, with more complex reactions to events (Schulz, 1982) and more complex experience of and ability to control emotional states (LaBouvie-Vief, DeVoe and Bulka, 1989). De Rivera (1984) argued for the development of a greater range of emotions and greater experience of the transformation of emotions as a likely outcome of increased experience throughout life.

Increased androgyny (Gutmann, 1987; Bengtson, Reedy and Gordon, 1985) can also be seen as increased psychological maturity. As one moves into the second half of life, behavior and social skills can become less constricted by sex role stereotypes and therefore more fully human. At least in the context of heterosexual relationships, men and women learn skills and behaviors from one another over a period of decades.

The mechanism for such improvement can be as simple (and as complex) as the accumulation of life experiences that can be understood as an increasingly complex database of human interaction. Breytspraak (1984) summarizes sociological and social psychological thought on the development of the self and notes that social comparison processes, reflected appraisals, and the role of person-environment interactions provide input for a dynamically evolving self-concept. The assumption that such input is continual throughout life implies that with increasing years, there is at least the potential for greater self-knowledge and the development of a more complex self (see also Markus and Herzog, 1991; Sherman, 1991).

Attacking the same notion from a somewhat different theoretical position, Bowen's family systems theory (see Hall, 1981) relates the development of the differentiated self to experience within one's family context. Bowen's concept of multigenerational transmission implies a general consistency from family of origin to family of marriage. Working with older families drives home the point that all older adults experience several family constellations: the family of origin, the family of marriage and small children, the extending family with adult children and grandchildren, and the dispersed family of later life. If one adds the knowledge gained of the spouse's family and the families of the spouses of the client's children, every older person can be something of an expert on family dynamics or, at least, someone who has experienced a wide range of family forms and issues.

In summary, these trends in gerontological thinking suggest a potential for continual growth toward maturity throughout the adult life span. In this sense, maturity means increasing cognitive complexity, possibly including postformal reasoning; development of expertise in areas of experiential competence including work, family, and relationships; androgyny, at least in the sense of acquiring role competencies and interests stereotypically associated with the opposite gender; and a greater emotional complexity with better comprehension and control of emotional reactions.

SPECIFICITY OF CHALLENGES IN LATE LIFE

Practitioners working with older adults may well be thinking at this juncture that this view of maturation throughout adulthood is overly optimistic. This outline of evidence for increasing maturation intentionally focused on normal development through the life span. Many elderly clients seeking help in therapy are struggling with problems that threaten psychological homeostasis at any point in the life span: chronic illness, disability, and the death of loved ones. Although not unique to late life, these problems are more likely to occur in the latter third of life. In addition, late life is not immune to the usual vicissitudes of all of life: disappointment in love, arguments with family members, and failing at the tasks we set ourselves. Finally, many people who have struggled with depression, anxiety, substance abuse, or psychosis all their lives eventually become older adults and are still struggling with these problems.

The specific nature of these problems is important to the practice of psychotherapy with individual older persons. Just as the deficit side of the loss-deficit model ignores evidence for maturation, the perception that generic losses are normative in late life fails to do justice to the specific nature of the losses incurred. Clinical experience suggests that it matters whether what is lost is one's spouse, one's vision, or the use of one's legs. Recognizing the specificity of loss and reconceptualizing losses as challenges implies that people can overcome some losses—through rehabilitation counseling, for example—and can adjust to others—for example, through grief counseling. Turning from a loss-deficit model to a maturity-specific challenge model also helps us to recognize when depression is not normative for a given life experience. For example, depression following retirement may be seen in this model as atypical (since many older adults enjoy freedom from the demands of work) and therefore in need of careful therapeutic assessment.

Table 12.1 The Maturity-Specific Challenge Model

Elements of Maturity	Specific Challenges
Cognitive complexity	Chronic illnesses
Postformal reasoning	Disabilities
Emotional complexity	Preparation for dying
Androgyny	Grieving for loved ones
Expertise	
Areas of competency	
Multiple family experiences	
Accumulated interprsonal skills	
	Contexts
Cohort Effects	Age-segregated
Cognitive abilities	communities
Education	Aging services agencies
Word usage	Senior recreation sites
Values	Medical settings
Normative life paths	Long-term care
Social-historical life	Age-based law and
experience	regulations

COHORT SPECIFICITY

Scientific gerontology makes another contribution to understanding older adults through developmental methodologies that separate the effects of maturation from the effects of cohort membership and social change. Much of social gerontology could be summarized as the discovery that many differences between the old and the young that society has attributed to the aging process are due, in fact, to cohort effects.

Cohort differences are explained by membership in a birth-year-defined group that is socialized into certain beliefs, attitudes, and personality dimensions that will stay constant as it ages and that distinguishes that cohort from those born earlier and later. For example, later-born cohorts in twentieth century America have more years of formal schooling than earlier-born groups. Research on cognitive abilities shows that later-born cohorts may be superior in spatial abilities and reasoning, whereas earlier-born cohorts may have the advantage in numerical abilities. Cohort comparisons are not always linear; some cognitive abilities (e.g., word fluency) have both improved and declined across successive cohorts (Schaie, 1983). Memory research has shown that earlier-born cohorts use "old words," and some differences between older people and younger people in learning word lists is eliminated if cohort-appropriate lists are used (see Botwinick, 1984). In other domains, social change that occurs before or during our childhood years may be taken for granted, but that which occurs during our adult years will be truly experienced as change.

These cohort differences are the reasons that older people seem "old-fashioned." Cohort effects and social change can also explain many of the misunderstandings that occur between young and old adults, including some of the failures in communication within families. Cohort differences in communication and in values complicate the interaction between earlier-born clients and later-born therapists. Earlier-born female clients may prefer to use words like irritated or frustrated to describe the emotion that later-borns call anger. Some later-born therapists feel that therapeutic breakthrough depends on using the word anger. On a different level, understanding what was normative for different cohorts can change the perceived meaning of life histories. The typical age of marriage varies by cohort. It can change the meaning of a life story to know whether someone who married "late" was from the World War I years or the Depression years (when many people delayed marriage to almost 1990s standards).

These differences, while not developmental, are real. Working with older adults involves learning something of the folkways of members of earlier-born cohorts, just as working with adolescents or young adults demands staying current in their folkways and worldview. During times of rapid social and technological change (the twentieth century comes to mind), cohort effects may overwhelm advantages of developmental maturation. Preparation to do therapy with older people has to include learning what it was like to grow up before we were born.

Understanding aging is about understanding maturation; working with old people is about understanding people who matured in a different era. Perhaps one of the most undeveloped aspects of understanding psychotherapy with older adults, namely, comprehending psychologically significant cohort effects, is not essentially different in quality or difficulty from learning to work with clients from other cultures or from the other gender.

THE SOCIAL CONTEXT OF OLDER ADULTS

A final complication for understanding older adults in psychotherapy is the need to understand the distinctive social milieu of older adults in the United States of the late twentieth century. This context includes specific environments (age-segregated housing, age-segregated social and recreational centers, the aging services network, age-segregated long-term care, and so on) as well as specific rules for older adults (Medicare regulations, Older Americans Act regulations, conservatorship law, and so forth). The network of aging services is yet another element of this context. An understanding of this social context that is based on both knowledge of what is supposed to be and experience of actual operations is important to the understanding of what clients say. A danger of selective exposure of professionals to these environments for older adults is that many people who are expert about a given context (e.g., skilled nursing facilities) imagine that they are expert about older adults in general.

Experience in training new therapists suggests that those student therapists without other contact with the social world of the elderly find the client's descriptions of this different world inordinately confusing. The social worlds of older and younger adults in our culture are sufficiently different that an accurate description of what goes on at a typical meal site can sound neurotic or even delusional to the uninitiated younger therapist. For example, an older client once described being anxious about being watched whenever she entered or left her HUD-subsidized apartment building. I wondered about her suspiciousness until I went to the same building to visit a different client and was scrutinized by two residents sitting by the elevator.

SUMMARY

Eight decades of case histories and a small number of controlled outcome studies suggest that psychotherapy with older adults is effective. There seems to be little reason to modify the goals, techniques, or the system of therapy used (Knight, 1986, 1992). The traditional loss-deficit model is overly generic in its conceptualization of loss and inaccurate in portraying normative aging as developing global deficits. A contextual, cohort-based maturity-specific challenge model is offered that can serve as a framework for applying theory and knowledge from gerontology to psychotherapy with older adults.

This article further develops ideas and duplicates material from the concluding chapter of Older Adults in Psychotherapy: Case Histories (Newbury Park, Calif.: Sage, 1992).

References

Bengtson, V. L., Reedy, M. N. and Gordon, C., 1985. "Aging and Self-Conceptions: Personality Processes and Social Contexts." In J. E. Birren and K. W. Schaie, eds., *Handbook of the Psychology of Aging*, 2d ed. New York: Van Nostrand Reinhold, pp. 544–93.

Botwinick, J., 1984. *Aging and Behavior*, 3d ed. New York: Springer Publishing Company.

Breytspraak, L. M., 1984. *The Development of Self in Later Life*. Boston, Mass.: Little, Brown.

Costa, P. T. et al., 1987. "Longitudinal Analysis of Psychological Well-being in a National Sample: Stability of Mean Levels." *Journal of Gerontology* 42: 50–56.

De Rivera, J., 1984. "Development and the Full Range of Emotional Expression." In C. Z. Malatesta and C. E. Izard, eds., *Emotion in Adult Development*. Beverly Hills, Calif.: Sage, pp. 45–63.

Gatz, M. and Hurwicz, M., 1990. "Are Older People More Depressed? Cross-sectional Data on Center for Epidemiological Studies Depression Scale

Factors." *Psychology and Aging* 5: 284–90.

Gutmann, D., 1987. *Reclaimed Powers: Toward a New Psychology of Men and Women in Later Life.* New York: Basic Books.

Gynther, M. D., 1979. "Aging and Personality." In J. N. Butcher, ed., *New Developments in the Use of the MMPI.* Minneapolis, Minn.: University of Minnesota Press, pp. 39–68.

Hall, C. M., 1981. *The Bowen Family Theory and Its Uses.* New York: Jason Aronson.

Knight, B. G., 1986. *Psychotherapy with the Older Adult.* Beverly Hills, Calif.: Sage.

Knight, B., 1992. *Older Adults in Psychotherapy: Case Histories.* Newbury Park, Calif.: Sage.

Knight, B., Kelly, M. and Gatz, M., 1992. "Psychotherapy with the Elderly." In D. K. Freedheim, ed., *The History of Psychotherapy.* Washington, D.C.: American Psychological Assn.

Labouvie-Vief, G., DeVoe, M. and Bulka, D., 1989. "Speaking About Feelings: Conceptions of Emotion Across the Life Span." *Psychology and Aging* 4(4): 425–37.

Markus, H. R. and Herzog, A. R., 1991. "The Role of the Self Concept in Aging." *Annual Review of Gerontology and Geriatrics* 11: 110–43.

Myers, J. K. et al., 1984. "Six-Month Prevalence of Psychiatric Disorders in Three Communities." *Archives of General Psychiatry* 41: 959–67.

Neugarten, B. L., 1977. "Personality and Aging." In J. E. Birren and K. W. Schaie, eds., *Handbook of the Psychology of Aging.* New York: Van Nostrand.

Rybash, J. M., Hoyer, W. J. and Roodin, P. A., 1986. *Adult Cognition and Aging.* New York: Pergamon Press.

Schaie, K. W., 1983. "The Seattle Longitudinal Study: A 21-Year Exploration of Psychometric Intelligence in Adulthood." In K. W. Schaie, ed., *Longitudinal Studies of Adult Psychological Development.* New York: Guilford, pp. 64–135.

Sherman, E., 1991. *Reminiscence and the Self in Old Age.* New York: Springer Publishing Company.

Schulz, R., 1982. "Emotionality and Aging: A Theoretical and Empirical Analysis." *Journal of Gerontology* 37: 42–51.

CHAPTER THIRTEEN

Mental Health and Aging

Federal Perspectives

Barry D. Lebowitz

n an issue of the American Society on Aging's journal devoted to public policy, I reviewed a number of concerns and challenges confronting the development of the field of mental health and aging (Lebowitz, 1988). This chapter addresses much of the same material but approaches the subject from a perspective informed by a number of recent developments. The theme used to organize this paper is one of mainstreaming—of concerns with aging within the mental health field and of concerns with mental health within the aging field. This theme of *mainstreaming* echoes and fully supports Gatz and Smyer (1992), who conclude their recently published overview with the proposition that in the 1990s, approaches to the mental health of older persons will necessarily and optimally be developed within a broad perspective rather than a narrow one focusing exclusively on that area.

In retrospect, all external indicators of the health and vitality of the field are positive. Basic and clinical research in the field is booming, and research centers are proliferating; new investigators are being attracted to the field, and postdoctoral training opportunities are being used to create the first generation of investigators prepared to launch academic research careers in mental health and aging. Built upon this growing and cumulative foundation of research-based knowledge, a number of specialized organizations of both national and international scope have been developed. Specialized scientific journals have also proliferated, and a greater number of general purpose journals will often contain articles of significance to mental health and aging. Major textbooks have been developed. Clinical training programs proliferate in all the mental health disciplines, and geriatric psychiatry is now a full-fledged subspecialty through added qualifications in psychiatry.

This was not always the case. There have been three phases in the evolution of interest in mental health and aging. The first phase was one in which the pioneers in the field were often confronted with the assertion that geriatric mental health was a "career buster" and that nothing of significance was possible in the field. It was often asserted that there was nothing interesting in caring for geriatric patients and there was nothing special that could be contributed to knowledge by developing research in the area. This perspective was very strongly in force until the early 1970s when the "discovery" of Alzheimer's disease legitimized limited aspects of the field. That is, the emergence of interest in Alzheimer's disease was seen as a proxy for all aging in both research and clinical programs. In other words, a "memory disorders clinic" or a "dementia research service" was seen as constituting all that was special in geriatrics—if Alzheimer's was covered, then so was all of aging.

Though continuing strongly in the field as a whole, the Alzheimer-only perspective is being replaced in the third phase of development of mental health and aging. In this phase, still very much in process, the boundaries of aging and mental health are seen to be as broad as the mental health field itself. Using either a life-course perspective on developmental psychopathology or a more direct, categorical approach to late-life mental disorders, we are now in the midst of a series of developments geared toward mainstreaming of concerns with aging within the overall mental health field.

Using the limited "convening" powers of the National Institute of Mental Health (NIMH), my colleagues and I have tried to support this development through a series of research conferences, workshops, and publications. Along with Alzheimer's disease (Light and Lebowitz, 1989; Light, Niederehe and Lebowitz, in press), we have developed projects in schizophrenia (Miller and Cohen, 1987; Light and Lebowitz, 1991), anxiety (Salzman and Lebowitz, 1990), delirium (Miller, Lipowski and Lebowitz, 1991), and depression (Schneider et al., in press).

The work in depression, which has been particularly noteworthy, was capped by a National Institutes of Health (NIH) Consensus Development Conference on Diagnosis and Treatment of Depression in Late Life held in late 1991. The overall outcome of the Consensus Development Conference is reviewed in another chapter of this issue. The process of consensus development is itself worthy of note, because it indicates that a body of scientific knowledge is strong enough for recommendations for nonspecialty clinical practice to be developed from this knowledge base. A certain level of maturation of a field and of an area is required before such a process can be initiated. There have been about 90 NIH Consensus Development Conferences in all areas of healthcare; this was the fifth to be sponsored by NIMH and the first to address late-life mental disorders.

The background material and recommendations of the Consensus Development Conference have been incorporated into a number of significant documents and processes such as the Clinical Practice Guidelines on Depression, under development at the federal Agency for Health Care Policy and Research, and the Treatment Guidelines for Depression, under development by the American Psychiatric Association. It is not inconceivable that just a few years ago these types of projects could have proceeded without any significant input from geriatrics. It is a mark of the increasing acceptance of our field that this geriatric input was solicited early in the process of guideline development.

The final step in the mainstreaming of research within the scientific establishment is contained in a legislative proposal to reorganize the federal Alcohol, Drug Abuse, and Mental Health Administration, the umbrella agency that houses NIMH, and to return NIMH as an institute of NIH. NIMH was one of the original institutes of NIH when it was established in the 1940s; expansion of responsibility in the institute to a variety of community service and training programs beyond its original research mission also required a variety of separate administrative arrangements for NIMH outside NIH. At times, these service and training responsibilities totally overshadowed the research mission of the institute; this, in turn, was reflected budgetarily over a long period in the 1960s and 1970s, during which appropriations for mental health research suffered relative to research support in other areas.

This relative shortfall in federal research support is all the more significant when viewed within the overall support picture for research in the field. Unlike other areas of health, such as cancer and heart disease, where an estimated 30–40 percent of the research support in the field comes from nonfederal sources, research in the mental and addictive disorders is overwhelmingly (90-plus percent) a matter for government support (Martinez, Lebowitz and Cohen, in press). Until such time as the foundations and voluntary agencies gain a greater foothold in our field, the mental health research structure is entirely too dependent upon public (i.e., federal) sources, with all the attendant uncertainties surrounding freezes, cuts, continuing resolutions, and budget balancing schemes.

The last decade has seen a variety of reconfigurations of federal support programs for mental health services and training of mental health clinical professionals, with the result that research has been reestablished as the primary mission of NIMH. The centrality of the research programs has, in turn, been reinforced by substantial increases in the appropriations for research. The level of support and the quality of the science is such that there is no reason to maintain the NIMH program as a separate, and some would infer thereby, inferior, component of the nation's health research enterprise. Consequently, in July 1992 the legislative proposal to move NIMH to NIH was approved overwhelmingly by the Senate and House of Representatives and signed into law by the President.

Now that the mainstreaming of research has been accomplished, the question remains as to whether this same logic will carry through to issues of mental health services and the reimbursement for these services. The clear linkage of these concerns was contained in the Senate bill on reorganization of NIMH (S. 1306), where a variety of studies are called for in order to set the stage for the even-handed inclusion of coverage for the mental disorders within any proposed program of national health insurance.

The reimbursement provided to mental health professionals for the treatment of mental disorders has always been problematic. Significant gaps in coverage have been allowed to develop, and reimbursement formulas, though improved, still maintain discriminatory distinctions between the mental disorders and all other disorders. There is a broad literature on this overall issue (see, for example, Fogel, Furino and Gottlieb, 1991), with all commentators usually concluding that mental health coverage is appropriate, necessary, and cost-effective.

These conclusions notwithstanding, the burden of proof remains a constant issue in the mental health field and will continue to be an area of paramount concern as the national health insurance debate develops over the next few years. The economic pressures are enormous and will continue to grow as the population ages and the chronically ill and disabled population survives into adulthood and old age. The total cost to American society of disorders of the brain and central nervous system has been estimated to be $401.1 billion (National Foundation for Brain Research, 1992). This astonishing figure, some 7.3 percent of Gross Domestic Product, includes over $104 billion spent for medical care alone, or approximately 14 percent of national healthcare expenditures. This level of need cannot be ignored in any rationally conceived reform of the healthcare system and associated healthcare financing developments. Consequently, the prospects for mainstreaming issues of finance and reimbursement of mental health care within an overall approach to healthcare financing appear to be positive, though far from definite.

The mainstreaming of mental health services within a universal system of health and social services remains a somewhat more complex issue. At one level, this is not a particularly pressing issue. There has been a long-held consensus in the field that geriatrics (in general) should not be viewed as pediatrics for the elderly. That is, the development of a free-standing, fully differentiated system of care strictly for older people, with legal sanction, as parallel to the present system, was never seen as a desirable outcome. In addition, a de facto system of mental health treatment within the primary care sector has emerged, with the result that most mental health care is provided outside the specialty mental health sector (George, 1992). It is probably the case that the closest approximation we have to a system in this country is the way primary care and specialty care operate in the mental health field. That is, most people who receive mental health care do so in the primary and nursing home sectors, although the appropriateness and adequacy of this care is highly variable. Only those with difficult diagnostic presentations, or who have not responded to first-line treatments, or (some would say) whom no one else wants to care for end up seeing a mental health provider at all. There are, of course, some special circumstances in which mental health specialty involvement is required, including assessment of competency as part of a guardianship or conservatorship proceeding, and, more recently, preadmission screening or annual review for nursing home placement.

For those who require the services of a geriatric mental health specialist, however, the identification of an appropriate professional or an appropriate setting can be problematic. With regard to setting, the availability and accessibility of specialized programs, public or private, are highly variable and often require some determined tracking. Owing to experiences with the stigma that, tragically, all too often accompanies mental disorders, many specialized programs adopt euphemisms as their titles ("geriatric family service," "creative aging") and thereby remain invisible to all but the most aware. In academic medical settings, nearly half the departments of psychiatry in the United States have some sort of geriatric psychiatry program—usually a fellowship with associated inpatient or outpatient services. Programs in clinical psychology of aging are, with a few significant exceptions, more likely to be found in psychiatry departments and medical centers of the Department of Veterans Affairs than in graduate or professional schools. In academic clinical psychology, social work, and psychiatric nursing, there are small handfuls of specialty clinical programs, and those seeking care would have to search diligently in order to find them.

With regard to specialist professionals, only psychiatry has subspecialization, through examination and fellowship for "added qualifications" in geriatrics. The matter has been under discussion by professionals in clinical psychology, with movement now in the field toward the development of special competency in geriatrics. For now, however, specialization and expertise in geriatrics can be asserted by the nonpsychiatrist mental health professional simply by purchasing an advertisement in the Yellow Pages, and there would be no basis upon which the potential user of the service could independently confirm the claimed expertise. We have reached an important transition point in professional expertise, however. Leaders in all the mental health disciplines are now calling for expertise and competence in geriatrics rather than sensitization and "gerontologizing" curricula. This is a positive development; with proper support from the field, it will lead to a significant improvement in mental health services for older persons.

Many of these developments have been facilitated by the establishment of the Coalition on Mental Health and Aging, a group convened by the American Association of Retired Persons and including representatives of over 30 national professional, provider, and citizen organizations in mental health and aging. As the coalition gains strength and visibility, we can expect that it will continue to vigorously pursue a national agenda in all aspects of mental health and aging. By its establishment, it has succeeded in placing aging in a place of prominence for mental health organizations and, conversely, in placing mental health in a priority position on the agenda of national organizations concerned with aging. (See chapter 19 for a more detailed discussion of the coalition.)

The field of mental health and aging has come a long way since the early period and is moving toward a mainstream status on the national agenda. This developmental process, though highly successful to this point, is far from complete. All of us must do everything necessary to maintain this positive momentum as we approach the many challenges to be confronted in the 1990s. We should settle for nothing less.

Acknowledgments

The judgments and opinions contained in this paper are personal and do not reflect official positions of the United States Government.

References

Fogel, B. S., Furino, A. and Gottlieb, G. L., eds., 1991. *Mental Health Policy for Older Americans.* Washington DC: American Psychiatric Press.

Gatz, M. and Smyer, M. A., 1992. "The Mental Health System and Older Adults in the 1990's." *American Psychologist* 47: 741–51.

George, L. K., 1992. "Community and Homecare for Mentally Ill Older Adults." In J. E. Birren, R. B. Sloane and G. D. Cohen, eds., *Handbook of Mental Health and Aging, 2nd ed.* San Diego, CA: Academic Press.

Lebowitz, B. D., 1988. "Mental Health Policy and Aging." *Generations* 12(3): 53–56.

Light, E. and Lebowitz, B. D., eds., 1989. *Alzheimer's Disease Treatment and Family Stress.* Washington, DC: Government Printing Office.

Light, E. and Lebowitz, B. D., eds., 1991. *The Elderly with Chronic Mental Illness.* New York: Springer Publishing Company.

Light, E., Niederehe, G. and Lebowitz, B. D., eds., in press. *Alzheimer's Disease and Family Stress.* New York: Springer Publishing Company.

Martinez, R. A., Lebowitz, B. D. and Cohen, G. D., in press. "Funding Research Structures." *International Journal of Geriatric Psychiatry.*

Miller, N. E. and Cohen, G. D., eds., 1987. *Schizophrenia and Aging.* New York: Guilford Press.

Miller, N. E., Lipowski, Z. J. and Lebowitz, B. D., eds., 1991. "Delirium: Advances in Research and Clinical Practice." *International Psychogeriatrics* 3(2).

National Foundation for Brain Research, 1992. *The Cost of Disorders of the Brain.* Washington D. C.: National Foundation.

Salzman, C., and Lebowitz, B. D., eds., 1990. *Anxiety in the Elderly.* New York: Springer Publishing Company.

Schneider, L. S. et al., eds., in press. *Diagnosis and Treatment of Depression in Late Life.* Washington, DC: American Psychiatric Press.

CHAPTER FOURTEEN

Mental Health and Managed Care for the Elderly

Issues and Options

Terrie Wetle

T he term *managed care* has been used to describe several different models of organizing and financing health services. The concept of managed care encompasses comprehensive models like health maintenance organizations as well as more targeted tools such as case management, preadmission screening, and concurrent review. As managed care tools have been increasingly applied to care of the general population, so too have they been considered and used in efforts to control utilization and costs of care for older persons. This chapter describes several of the more popular models and tools of managed care and reviews the potential advantages and concerns for their application to the mental health care of older populations.

PREPAID, CAPITATED PROGRAMS

Health maintenance organizations (HMOs) integrate traditional insurance and the healthcare delivery function into one organization. HMOs share four basic features: (1) contractual responsibility for assuring delivery of a stated range of services, (2) a voluntarily enrolled population, (3) fixed monthly payment for enrollees independent of use of services, and (4) assumption of financial risk or gain (Luft, 1981). Based upon early plans for Los Angeles city workers in 1929 and Kaiser construction workers in the late 1930s, the Federal H.M.O. Act (P.L. 93-222) was passed in 1973. There are three models of HMOs: the

Staff/Group model, in which the HMO employs physicians to provide services exclusively to plan enrollees; the *Closed Panel*, in which physicians contract to provide services to enrollees on a capitated basis but may serve other patients as well; and the *Independent Practice Association* (IPA), in which physicians work in their own settings but bill the IPA on a discounted fee-for-service or capitated basis (Luft, 1981).

It has been argued that HMOs achieve cost-savings as compared to the fee-for-service system and that these cost-savings are based on several factors, including the following: (1) removal of financial incentives to overprovide service; (2) addition of a financial incentive to maintain enrollee health and thereby decrease utilization; and (3) managing care so that less expensive services are substituted for more expensive ones (e.g., substituting outpatient for inpatient treatment or substituting lower-paid workers for physicians) (Bonanno and Wetle, 1984). Indeed, experience indicates that major cost-savings are achieved primarily through reductions in hospital utilization, which is 15 to 40 percent less than found in the fee-for-service system (Luft, 1981). Although it has been argued that these savings are attributable to the enrollment of healthier populations into HMOs, randomized studies comparing the cost and utilization experience of HMOs and various fee-for-service plans suggest that annual expenditures, hospital admission rates, and total hospital days are significantly lower in HMOs compared to the fee-for-service plans, even when controlling for the health status of patients (Manning et al., 1984).

MEDICARE INVOLVEMENT IN PREPAID CAPITATED PROGRAMS

Although some Medicare beneficiaries were enrolled in prepaid health plans in the 1960s, the plans were reimbursed only for Part B services on a noncapitated basis (Iglehart, 1985). Since 1972, Medicare has permitted direct, capitated prepayment to HMOs for both Part A and Part B, and in 1982 Congress, in the Tax Equity and Fiscal Responsibility Act (TEFRA), authorized that prepaid care be available to all elders by amending the Social Security Act to allow prospective capitation payments at 95 percent of the average Medicare costs for beneficiaries of the same age and sex living in that community (Schlesinger and Drumheller, 1988). In 1991, 208 of the 581 HMOs accepted Medicare enrollees, accounting for 2,170,000 enrollees, up from 1,896,000 Medicare enrollees in 1990 (*Managed Care Digest,* 1992).

There are several *potential* advantages to enrolling Medicare beneficiaries into HMOs. Cost-containment could lead to overall savings for the Medicare program as well as to improved services to the elderly, if indeed savings are converted into added benefits. In the past, when such cost-savings have occurred, HMOs have chosen either to reduce copayment requirements for enrollees or to cover ancillary medical expenses; for example, for eyeglasses, dental care, or prescription drugs (Iglehart, 1985; Rossiter, Friedlob and Langwell, 1985; Ellwood, 1986). Moreover, the centralized record keeping and administrative systems of HMOs provide enhanced opportunities for improved case management, particularly for elderly patients with chronic diseases and multiple health problems (Bonanno and Wetle, 1984). Unfortunately, although some HMOs have developed case management systems for Medicare enrollees, most Medicare HMO programs have fallen short of developing systems particularly suited to the needs of elderly people (Iversen and Polich, 1985; Schlesinger, 1986). Special demonstrations of "enhanced" HMOs such as the social health maintenance organization (SHMO) projects supported by the Health Care Financing Administration over the past several years indicate that it *is* possible to develop models of care with a broad array of needed services, but that such models are likely to have substantial start-up costs (Greenberg et al., 1988).

Capitated plans for special populations are even more limited. The On Lok Senior Health Services project in San Francisco has served a population of heavily impaired elderly, providing an array of primary care and acute and long-term health and social services (Hamm, Kickham and Cutler, 1982). Over several years, the On Lok project has developed agreements with public payers under which Medicare, Medicaid, and the enrollee each pay a "premium" based on the individual's entitlement. On Lok bears 100 percent of the financial risk for the complete care of its locked-in census. Cost-efficiency is achieved in the On Lok program through a strikingly low use of hospitals and nursing homes (1percent and 3 percent respectively), via an emphasis on daycare, home services, and innovative housing arrangements. Efforts to replicate the On Lok model are under way at several sites across the country.

MENTAL HEALTH BENEFITS AND UTILIZATION IN PREPAID PLANS

In general, HMOs have offered Medicare enrollees the equivalent of the standard Medicare mental health benefit. There is a rather marked distinction, however, between the benefit package offered and actual utilization of services. Several factors limit use of mental health services by Medicare enrolless, including administrative policies that discourage use of service.

Few data exist regarding the use of psychiatric services by HMO *Medicare enrollees*, but studies of *general* (i.e., nonelderly) HMO enrollee utilization are informative. Although some early studies indicated higher use of mental health services among HMO enrollees than among fee-for-service patients, more recent studies indicate lower or similar utilization rates for HMO enrollees (Norquist and Wells, 1991). There does, however, appear to be a substitution of lower-cost personnel (nonpsychiatrists) and sites of service (outpatient) for HMO enrollees. Developing a clear understanding of HMO utilization is complicated by the observation that patients with higher levels of *general* health-service utilization are more likely to report psychiatric or mental health symptoms (McFarland et al., 1985; Waxman, Carner and Blum, 1983), but are not likely to be treated for mental illness; if they do receive treatment, it is likely to be by non-mental-health professionals. Focusing simply on psychiatric services within the HMO will provide a biased underestimate of overall service use by patients with mental health service needs.

OTHER MANAGED CARE TOOLS

HMOs and other forms of prepaid, capitated programs are not the only managed care tools in use. Several of these tools have more to do with "cost-containment" than with "managing" the care of patients.

Diagnosis-Related Groups

DRGs reimburse inpatient care based on diagnostic categories rather than on length of stay. DRGs have proven to be such a poor predictor of length of psychiatric stay that they have been excluded from the system (Schumacher et al., 1986). Research is under way, however, to develop such a model for mental health services.

Precertification and Concurrent Review Programs

These are two models that have been adopted across the country. It is estimated that virtually all third-party payers conduct or sponsor some type of utilization review (Ermann, 1988). Precertification is a mandatory prior-approval program that certifies all admissions as medically necessary before or within 24 hours after admission, authorizing a certain number of days to be reimbursed. Precertification, while of growing importance for general medical admissions, has been of limited value in curtailing unnecessary psychiatric admissions, primarily because of the scarcity of objective diagnostic data regarding both specific diagnosis and severity of illness for psychiatric admissions (Wetle and Mark, 1990).

Mandatory concurrent review programs subject all psychiatric and substance abuse admissions to the scrutiny of concurrent review, specific to treatment and discharge planning, with a focus on reducing length of stay. A recent study of general medical services concluded that such programs reduce inpatient days by 8 percent and hospital costs by almost 12 percent (Feldstein, Wickizew and Wheeler, 1988). Such efforts, however, are increasingly controversial. The American Hospital Association noted in 1988 that the Mayo Clinic was responding to more than a thousand private review agencies and went on to assert that "using the utilization review function to camouflage arbitrary coverage restrictions can lead to clinical standards set by insurance agents rather than by qualified clinicians" (American Hospital Association, 1988). Concurrent review procedures applied to psychiatric patients suffer from the same data deficiencies that hinder precertification efforts. Nonetheless, Medicare, through its representatives, continues to review patient charts looking for "key phrases" that indicate the necessity for continued hospitalization.

Case Management

This is also an important managed care tool with particular relevance for the elderly psychiatric patient. Unfortunately, the term "case management" has been used to describe several different and potentially competing functions including concurrent review, a gate-keeping function, as well as client advocacy and direct hands-on coordination of services (Wetle, 1988; Wetle and Mark, 1990).

Carve-Out Arrangements

A rapidly growing managed care trend relative to specialty services is what is known as a carve-out. A carve-out usually involves a discount in exchange for priority or sole access to an enrolled population for specific services such as pharmacy, rehabilitation, or mental health. For the elderly mentally ill, carve-outs may offer a greater likelihood of receiving more specialized care. There have, however, been concerns raised regarding psychiatric carve-outs. One problem is the potential loss of coordination between the more traditional medical services and the psychiatric services offered via carve-out arrangements. This may be a particular problem for elderly patients, who are more likely to have comorbidities and to suffer adverse drug reactions.

POTENTIAL BENEFITS

The "managed care revolution" (*Health Affairs*, 1988) holds some promise for older persons. Although Medicare is a major player relative to healthcare services for the elderly, it does not now adequately serve the needs of those who are mentally ill. For the elderly mentally ill to benefit directly from Medicare reform, we must address the issue of responsibility for care among levels of government. Shifting of patients (and costs) from one public payer to another will continue until there is clear public policy coordinating state and federal service payment. One promising approach to this dilemma is suggested by the On Lok demonstrations, which "pool" public moneys from Medicare, Medicaid, and state funds. Quality of care, coordination of services, cost, and quality of life indicators all require monitoring, but such a demonstration suggests that it is possible to better serve this population by rebundling services and funding. The reluctance of policy makers to comprehensively address the full array of services required by elderly persons might also be eased if managed care "tools" are shown to be effective in controlling costs and assuring quality of care.

PROBLEMS AND CONCERNS

Managed care does, however, involve certain risks for older persons. By introducing a centralized organizational focus and a management control function, it is assumed that inefficiencies will be reduced and the money saved can be redirected to other services, such as social supports. This assumption must be tested and supported before being globally adopted. It may well be that even if the management function is superior, we may discover that the inefficiencies we are counting on reducing to provide the "margin" are not there. There is evidence that the elderly underutilize psychiatric services (Frisman and McGuire, 1989). If so, then the fat in the system that can be eliminated to reduce costs is limited, and budgets may be met by restricting access to services. Furthermore, as overall costs in the system increase, managed care models and tools may be used to further restrict care for an already underserved population.

Achieving the promise offered by managed care models requires diligence and increased attention to advocacy and quality assurance. Moreover, we must redouble our efforts to improve coordination among service providers and payers for those services.

Acknowledgments

The author wishes to thank Hal Mark, Ph.D., University of Connecticut Health Center, for his collaboration on the preparation of an earlier manuscript on this topic.

References

American Hospital Association, 1988. *Statement on Private Utilization Review Before the Institute of Medicine.* Washington, DC, June 6.

Bonanno, J. B. and Wetle, T. W., 1984. "HMO Enrollment of Medicare Recipients: An Analysis of Incentives and Barriers." *Journal of Health Politics, Policy and Law* 9: 41–62.

Ellwood, D. A., 1986. "Medicare Risk Contracting: Promise and Problems." *Health Affairs* 5: 183–89.

Ermann, D., 1988. "Hospital Utilization Review: Past Experience, Future

Directions." *Journal of Health Politics, Policy and Law* 13: 683–704.

Feldstein, P. J., Wickizew, T. M. and Wheeler, J. C., 1988. "The Effects of Utilization Review Programs on Health Care Use and Expenditures." *New England Journal of Medicine* 318(20): 1310–14.

Frisman, L. K. and McGuire, T. C., 1989. "The Economics of Long-Term Care for the Mentally Ill." *Journal of Social Issues* 45(3): 119–30.

Greenberg, J. et al., 1988. "The Social HMO Demonstration: Early Experience." *Health Affairs* 7: 66–79.

Hamm, L., Kickham, T. and Cutler, D., 1982. "Research, Demonstrations and Evaluations." In R. Vogel and H. Palmer, eds., *Long-Term Care: Perspectives from Research and Demonstrations.* Washington, DC: Health Care Financing Administration, U.S. Department of Health and Human Services.

Health Affairs, 1988, 7(3). Entire issue devoted to managed care.

Iglehart, J. K., 1985. "Medicare Turns to HMOs." *New England Journal of Medicine* 312(2): 132–36.

Iversen, L. H. and Polich, C. L., 1985. *The Future of Medicare and HMOs.* Excelsior, MN: Interstudy.

Luft, H., 1981. *Health Maintenance Organizations: Dimensions of Performance.* New York: John Wiley.

Managed Care Digest, 1992. Kansas City, MO: Marion, Merrell, Dow.

Manning, W.G. et al., 1984. "A Controlled Trial of the Effect of a Prepaid Group Practice on the Use of Services." *New England Journal of Medicine* 310: 1505–10.

McFarland, B. H. et al., 1985. "Utilization Patterns Among Long Term Enrollees in a Prepaid Group Practice HMO." *Medical Care* 23: 1221.

Medicine and Health, 1988. "Champus Psychiatric Reforms Draw Fire." *Perspectives.* July 18.

Norquist G. S. and Wells, K. B., 1991. "How Do HMOs Reduce Outpatient Mental Health Care Costs?" *American Journal of Psychiatry* 148: 96–101.

Rossiter, L., Friedlob, A. and Langwell, K., 1985. "Exploring Benefits of Risk-based Contracting Under Medicare." *Health Care Financing Review* 39: 42–57.

Schlesinger, M., 1986. "On the Limits of Expanding Health Care Reform: Chronic Care in Proper Settings." *Milbank Quarterly* 64(2): 189.

Schlesinger, M. and Drumheller, P. B., 1988. "Medicare and Innovative Insurance Plans." In D. Blumenthal, M. Schlesinger and P. B. Drumheller, eds., *Renewing the Promise: Medicare and Its Reform.* New York: Oxford University Press.

Schumacher, D. N. et al., 1986. "Prospective Payment for Psychiatry—Feasibility and Impact." *New England Journal of Medicine* 315(21): 1331–36.

Waxman, H., Carner, E. and Blum, A., 1983. "Depressive Symptoms and Health Service Utilization Among the Community Elderly." *Journal of the American Geriatrics Society* 31: 417–20.

Wetle, T., 1988. "The Social and Service Context of Geriatric Care." In J. W. Rowe and R. W. Besdine, eds., *Geriatric Medicine.* Boston: Little, Brown.

Wetle, T. and Mark, H., 1990. "Managed Care." In B. S. Fogel, A. Furino and G. L. Gottlieb, eds., *Mental Health Policy for Older Americans: Protecting Minds at Risk.* Washington, DC: American Psychiatric Press.

Family Therapy with Older Adults

Sara Honn Qualls

ervice providers in housing, healthcare, and social services frequently encounter families who need assistance with the transitions of later life. Many families simply need information. Others need more intensive intervention in the form of family therapy. This chapter describes the structures of later life families, challenges faced by these families, and strategies for family assessment and therapy (see also Qualls, 1991).

The changing demographic structure of society affects the shape of later life families (Hagestad, 1988). Changes in life expectancy, fertility rates, participation of women in the work force, rates of divorce and remarriage—all have an impact on family structures. Currently, three- and four-generation families are commonplace. Each generation has fewer participants, thus creating a "beanpole structure" with more vertical than horizontal ties. Divorces and remarriages add complex lines of relatedness to the family tree. Each of these changes adds to the complexity of family interactions.

The new family structures influence the ways families relate. Family members may now spend several decades in each relationship. Middle generations have responsibilities to both the younger and the older generations, a potentially stressful position. Women particularly feel this strain as they juggle multiple family roles while participating in the work force. Family members of distant generations retain contact but have ambiguous roles (e.g., what is the role of a great-granddaughter-in-law?). Families must figure out how to meet members' needs while their roles are in transition.

Families primarily seek intervention to assist with parent–child relationships in which one generation needs assistance from another (for description of marital therapy, see Wolinsky, 1990; Qualls, in press). Parents caring for a dysfunctional (e.g., mentally retarded) or distressed (e.g., experiencing midlife divorce or financial loss) child may need assistance with setting appropriate boundaries on their roles or with long-term planning (Florsheim and Herr, 1990). Adult children concerned about aging parents may need help identifying the parents' need for assistance. For example, previously abused children may be hesitant to recognize that their father's incompetence is due to a biological disease rather than capricious irresponsibility. Other children may provide their parents with services that are not needed. Sibling conflict over parent care can also prompt a family to seek assistance.

Assessment of families begins with comprehensive assessment of the elderly members' physical and mental health (Lawton, 1986). This step provides a clear picture of older members' functional competence, knowledge needed to ensure that assigned roles are appropriate.

Decisions about whom to include in the family assessment are tailored to the specific family situation. Who is involved in the problem? Who has power in the family? Who provides key services to the identified patient? Telephone interviews, family sessions during holiday periods when more members are present, and individual sessions may all be useful tools (Duffy, 1986).

One key issue is to clarify a behavioral definition of the problem (Herr and Weakland, 1979). For whom is it a problem? What is the context of the problem (place, time, setting)? Who perceives it as a problem? How did the family seek assistance?

Another key issue is to identify what solutions the family has already attempted. Families' previous efforts to solve the problem are often important factors in the maintenance of the problem (Herr and Weakland, 1979).

A genogram depicting family relationships is extremely helpful in identifying family members, important family historical events, and family structure (McGoldrick and Gerson, 1985; Walsh, 1988). When discussing the genogram, families can describe previous successes and failures in coping with life events, and the therapist can then use these earlier experiences to guide current problem-solving.

Intervention strategies with later life families are generally similar to those used with younger couples. Traditional interventions used with older families include problem-focused interventions (Herr and Weakland, 1979), communication instruction (Patten and Piercy, 1989), paradoxical interventions (Gafner, 1987; Gilewski, Kuppinger and Zarit, 1985), cognitive-behavioral interventions (Pinkston and Linsk, 1984; Qualls, 1988), therapy using Bowen theory (Quinn and Keller, 1981), life review (Hargraves and Anderson, 1992; Wolinsky, 1990), and education about the transition (e.g., caregiving interventions include education about the disease, strategies for solving disease-specific problems, and strategies for obtaining resources and support for the disease process) (Zarit, Orr and Zarit, 1985; Zarit and Teri, 1991). Unique aspects of working with later life families center primarily around issues related to the health and functional status of eldest members (as noted above), the longevity and complexity of family history, and changing power structures in the family because of aging (Bonjean, 1988).

In summary, clinical work with aging families requires an understanding of family structure and function. Assessment and intervention have much in common with therapy with younger families, with unique aspects centering around health problems and the history of the relationships. A growing clinical literature offers several different approaches to assist therapists in developing options for successful intervention.

References

Bonjean, M. J., 1988. "Adult Children and Their Parents." *Convergence in Aging* 4: 100–111.

Duffy, M., 1986. "The Techniques and Contexts of Multigenerational Therapy." In T. L. Brink, ed., *Clinical Gerontology: A Guide to Assessment and Intervention.* New York: Haworth.

Florsheim, M. J. and Herr, J. J., 1990. "Family Counseling with Elders." *Generations* 14(1): 40–42.

Gafner, G., 1987. "Paradoxical Marital Therapy and the Discouragement Meter." *Clinical Gerontologist* 6(3): 67–70.

Gilewski, M. J., Kuppinger, J. and Zarit, S. H., 1985. "The Aging Marital System: A Case Study in Life Changes and Paradoxical Interventions." *Clinical Gerontologist* 3(3): 3–15.

Hagestad, G. O., 1988. "Demographic Change and the Life Course: Some Emerging Trends in the Family Realm." *Family Relations* 37: 405–10.

Hargraves, T. D. and Anderson, W. T., 1992. *Finishing Well: Aging and Reparation in the Intergenerational Family.* New York: Brunner/Mazel.

Herr, J. J. and Weakland, J. H., 1979. *Counseling Elders and Their Families.* New York: Springer Publishing Company.

Lawton, M. P., 1986. "Functional Assessment." In L. Teri and P. M. Lewinsohn, eds., *Geropsychological Assessment and Treatment.* New York: Springer Publishing Company.

McGoldrick, M. and Gerson, R., 1985. *Genograms in Family Assessment.* New York: Norton.

Patten, P. C. and Piercy, F. P., 1989. "Dysfunctional Isolation in the Elderly: Increasing Marital and Family Closeness Through Improved Communication." *Contemporary Family Therapy* 11: 131–47.

Pinkston, E. M. and Linsk, N. L., 1984. *Care of the Elderly: A Family Approach.* New York: Pergamon.

Qualls, S. H., 1988. "Problems in Families of Older Adults." In N. Epstein, S. E. Schlesinger and W. Dryden, eds., *Cognitive-Behavioral Therapy with Families.* New York: Brunner-Mazel.

Qualls, S. H., 1991. "Therapy with Older Families." In P. Keller, ed., *Innovations in Clinical Practice: A Source Book, Vol. 10.* Sarasota, FL: Professional Resource Exchange.

Qualls, S. H., in press. "Marital Therapy with Older Couples." *The Family Journal.*

Quinn, W. H. and Keller, J. F., 1981. "A family Therapy Model for Preserving Independence in Older Persons: Utilization of the Family of Procreation." *American Journal of Family Therapy* 9: 79–84.

Walsh, F., 1988. "The Family in Later Life." In B. Carter and M. McGoldrick, eds., *The Changing Family Life Cycle.* New York: Gardner.

Wolinsky, M. A., 1990. *A Heart of Wisdom: Marital Counseling with Older and Elderly Couples.* New York: Brunner/Mazel.

Zarit, S. H., Orr, N. K. and Zarit, J. M., 1985. *The Hidden Victims of Alzheimer's Disease: Families Under Stress.* New York: New York University Press.

Zarit, S. H. and Teri, L., 1991. "Interventions and Services for Family Caregivers." *Annual Review of Gerontology and Geriatrics, Vol. 11*: New York: Springer Publishing Company, pp. 287–310.

Adult Daycare for Persons with Dementia

A Viable Community Option

Marilyn Engstrom, Rickey Greene, and Mary Casey O'Connor

dult daycare is a viable option in the long-term-care continuum of care for persons with Alzheimer's disease and other dementias. Programs have flourished in the last few years as families trying to maintain their family member with dementia at home have looked to the community for help. They have looked for help in providing quality care for their family member and for some respite from their own difficult and stressful caregiving responsibilities. The experience of the State of New Jersey illustrates the components necessary for successfully developing and implementing adult daycare.

New Jersey's efforts to develop a continuum of care for Alzheimer's disease date back to 1983 with the establishment of the New Jersey Alzheimer's Disease Study Commission. The commission estimated that approximately 180,000 New Jersey residents have a form of dementia. In its Final Report in 1986, the commission recommended that the state provide support for the development of a diagnostic center, an information and referral center, expansion of adult daycare programs, and training and educational materials for family caregivers and professionals.

As a result of the daycare recommendation, legislation was introduced, and an appropriation of $1.1 million was made to the Department of Health in July 1987 to develop a statewide program to provide adult daycare services for victims of Alzheimer's disease.

Working closely with the Alzheimer's Association and the New

Jersey Adult Day Care Association, a Request for Applications form was developed and mailed to all medical and social adult daycare centers statewide, totaling approximately one hundred at the time. Twenty-eight agencies are currently receiving letters of agreement for service.

To be eligible for the Dementia Day Care Program, an older adult must meet the following criteria:

1. Have a diagnosis, documented by a licensed physician, of Alzheimer's disease or one of the related dementias.
2. Be routinely supervised by an informal caregiver.
3. Reside in the community, but not in a rooming house or boarding home.
4. Have documented evidence of eligibility according to income guidelines.
5. Be a resident of the State of New Jersey.

After a client's eligibility for service has been established, agency personnel complete further assessments and develop a treatment plan that identifies both immediate and long-range goals for both the dementia victim and his or her caregiver. Implementation varies from agency to agency, since some maintain totally separate programs for clients with dementia, some are partially integrated, and others are totally integrated. Within a safe, supervised environment, staff incorporate physical, social, cognitive, and functional activities to maximize remaining strengths and minimize deficits. Exercise, music, and forms of reminiscence, reality orientation, and remotivation are included in the daily routines of most of the programs. All provide a noon meal and snacks, and the majority furnish transportation. Services to caregivers include counseling, referral, educational programs, and support groups.

Clients are provided two to five days of service per week, depending on the need and availability of funds. From November 1987, when service began, through June 1992, a total of 999 clients have received 111,849 days of service. The average per diem cost to the state was $33.59 in fiscal year 1992. Currently, 198 persons throughout the state are receiving subsidized service. Given our present budget, we are unable to enroll additional clients until another client is discharged. Therefore, a waiting list for service exists.

Because most programs are relatively small with a high client/staff ratio, they are able to provide highly individualized care to clients and their family members. In addition to providing actual daycare, one of the most significant components of adult daycare service is case management. In a community service setting that is involved with the client/caregiver dyad nearly daily, the professional staff (registered nurse, social worker or program director) assume the role of case manager for all services or needs of the client with dementia and his or her caregiver.

Daycare staff are well acquainted with client/caregiver needs as well as resources available in their communities. Thus, they are able to efficiently and effectively match needs and services. These include in-home chore or homemaker–home health aides to assist the client with personal care in the morning, transportation services, legal or financial assistance, and referrals for healthcare problems.

Daycare staff also provide families with information essential to caregiving tasks in the home and problem solving. Their knowledge of the client and his or her particular behaviors makes it possible for daycare staff to do this on a highly personalized level.

In addition, staff members provide emotional support through either telephone or direct contact as often as needed. Frequently, for overburdened caregivers, this means daily. In many instances, agency staff share their home telephone numbers with caregivers of dementia victims, so staff are accessible in the evenings and on weekends. Their sense of commitment to providing quality care and service extends beyond that which would generally be expected.

More formal support is provided through support groups, which most adult daycare programs sponsor. These support groups have an education/support or self-help/support format. They often have the additional benefit of facilitating communication and supportive relationships between caregivers.

One daycare program took the initiative of developing a county-wide support group for Alzheimer's caregivers in collaboration with other county agencies. In addition to sponsoring the support group, they opened the doors of their daycare facility on Saturday afternoons to provide respite care during the hours of the support group meetings so that caregivers might more readily attend. This service was provided free of charge.

Most professionals involved in providing daycare service to victims of Alzheimer's disease and related disorders believe that adult daycare is beneficial to clients as well as caregivers. This has not been empirically validated through research studies, however. the Gerontology Program, in collaboration with Penn State and Kent State Universities, has recently received a five-year grant from the National Institute on Aging to determine whether caregiver stress is reduced by the provision of adult daycare services. The results of our study should offer directions for further improvement of this valuable set of services.

Reference

New Jersey Alzheimer's Disease Study Commission, 1986. *Final Report.* Trenton: New Jersey State Department of Health.

CHAPTER SEVENTEEN

Preventive Interventions for Older Adults

Candace Stacey-Konnert

T he importance of a proactive, preventive approach to mental health problems has long been recognized by community psychologists. Unfortunately, there has been little overlap between community psychology and the psychology of aging and adult development. To illustrate, Buckner et al. (1985) compiled an annotated bibliography of primary prevention literature, and of 1,008 references, 26 dealt with older adults and only three were evaluated interventions.

The purpose of this chapter is to present some general observations on the status of prevention efforts among older adults. It is based on an in-depth review of the gerontological and community psychology literatures from 1980 until the present, focusing on those interventions which had the best empirical evaluation (Stacey-Konnert and Gatz, in press). Several trends emerged from this review. First, community psychologists typically distinguish among individual, family, community, and social policy levels of intervention, and most of the evaluated interventions were at the individual level. Although these are obviously worthwhile, interventions at the community and policy levels can potentially affect many more older adults.

Second, while the review revealed a wide range of preventive interventions, evaluated programs were few. Third, much of the research lacked a conceptual basis or was at least described in terms removed from a community psychology framework. For example, a major focus has been increasing social networks of "at risk" elders. Rationales for these programs are obvious and good, but the complexity of what is known about social support has not been transferred to planning interventions. All social support does not equally serve to build competence.

Fourth, the review showed that little attention has been paid to the possibility of unintended negative consequences or concern about which interventions might be best for which older adults. Older adults are a diverse group, and while some are poor or isolated, others feel busier than at any other time in their lives.

Fifth, although independent living was often a stated goal of programs discussed in the reviewed literature, models of intervention that actually incorporated considerations of autonomy and empowerment were rare. This is unfortunate because empowerment programs can foster a sense of efficacy by giving people control over decisions in their lives and can change the nature of the helping relationship to make it more symmetrical (Gesten and Jason, 1987; Hofland, 1988; Tyler, Pargament and Gatz, 1983). Such programs obviously deserve greater attention from program planners and community researchers. Of course, the issue of empowerment is inseparable from considerations of what is possible or available. Programs designed to foster autonomy must balance risk and protection, particularly for demented elderly. Also, prevention programs typically are neither fundable nor reimbursable (Bloom, 1985).

Clearly, the definition of prevention takes on some unique aspects when the target group is older adults. Although this review focused on interventions directed at those already aged, the prevention of mental health problems is a life-long process, and it is quite conceivable that some preventive efforts at much younger ages may actually have their strongest effects in old age. Consider that many individuals with troubled developmental histories have as younger or middle-aged adults managed to escape the notice of professionals but encounter obvious problems in their later years, when other vulnerabilities have made managing more difficult (Kral, 1968). Similarly, people who experience such difficulties as poverty, ill health or poor health habits, and marginal jobs are more likely to be dependent as elders (Hendricks and Leedham, 1989).

Moreover, one must beware of equating prevention of pathology in old age with prevention of old age. While this statement may sound foolishly simplistic, there is prevalent in this society a paradoxical view that to grow old well is to stay young. This view is a denial of normal development and should be rejected in favor of the goal of a fulfilled old age.

Furthermore, younger adults' "at risk" status refers to their vulnerability to psychological distress or mental illness. In contrast, older adults are often placed in an "at risk" category because of physical frailty that puts them at risk of being placed in a nursing home. Risk of mental distress is predominantly secondary to the threat of being placed in a long-term-care institution. A great deal of emphasis is thus placed on preventing institutionalization with, unfortunately, little emphasis on preventing psychological distress or mental illness.

In conclusion, two images of the older adult must inform preventive mental health approaches. One image is of the older person as extremely vital, planning new undertakings, conveying the wisdom built up over a lifetime. A second image is of the older person as realistically aware of the inevitable changes that limit his or her life, especially changes in physical health. The concept of empowerment has the capacity to encompass both of these images, and recognizes the need to match programs to persons. Thus the application of a community psychology conceptual framework to prevention in the lives of older adults sounds a hopeful note.

References

Bloom, B. L., 1985. "Focal Issues in the Prevention of Mental Disorders." In H. H. Goldman and S. E. Goldston, eds., *Preventing Stress-Related Psychiatric Disorders* Rockville, MD: National Institute of Mental Health, (DHHS Publication No. ADM 85-1336).

Buckner, J. C., Tricket, E. J. and Corse, J., 1985. *Primary Prevention in Mental Health: An Annotated Bibliography* Rockville, MD: National Institute of Mental Health, (DHHS Publication No. ADM 85-1405).

Gesten, E. L. and Jason, L. A., 1987. "Social and Community Interventions." *Annual Review of Psychology* 38: 427-60.

Hendricks, J. and Leedham, C. A., 1989. "Creating Psychological and Societal Dependency in Old Age." In P. S. Fry, ed., *Psychological Perspectives of Helplessness and Control in the Elderly*. New York: Elsevier Science.

Hofland, B. F., 1988. "Autonomy in Long Term Care: Background Issues and a Programmatic Response." *Gerontologist* 28(1): 3–9.

Kral, V. A., 1968. "Primary Prevention of Psychiatric Disorders." In F. C. R. Chalke and J. J. Day, eds., *Geriatric Psychiatry.* Toronto,ON: University of Toronto Press.

Stacey-Konnert, C. and Gatz M., in press. "Community and Preventive Interventions for Normative Occurrences of Later Life." In J. Rappaport and E. Seidman, eds., *The Handbook of Community Psychology.* New York: Plenum.

Tyler, F. B., Pargament, K. I. and Gatz, M., 1983. "The Resource Collaborator Role: A Model for Interactions Involving Psychologists." *American Psychologist* 38(4): 388–98.

Neuroimaging

Advances and New Directions

Larry Tune

dvances in neuroimaging techniques have permitted dramatic increases in our ability to investigate brain structure and function. These methods have recently been studied to determine their usefulness in establishing the diagnosis of Alzheimer's disease (AD). Since the clinical diagnosis of Alzheimer's disease can be as accurate as 90–95 percent, these techniques must be very accurate (>90 percent) to be of clinical value. The most promising advances of practical value to clinicians have come from studies using MRI (magnetic resonance imaging) to detect changes in brain structure, and SPECT (single photon emission computed tomography) to detect changes in cerebral function. Recent studies combining these two methods have offered even greater promise.

Many computerized tomographic (CT) studies have demonstrated regional and global cerebral atrophy in AD patients. However, in part because of age-related variability of brain size, there is considerable overlap between patients and controls. For this reason, this finding alone is of little diagnostic value. MRI has the advantage of providing much more exquisite structural detail, allowing for careful studies of regional brain anatomy. Recent studies (Pearlson et al., 1992; Bondareff et al., 1990) have identified discrete anatomic regions and illness-related macroscopic changes of particular relevance to AD. For example, Seab et al. (1988) and Pearlson et al. (1992) found significant structural changes (decreased cerebral volume) in AD patients in the mesial temporal lobe—a region known from postmortem studies to be affected in AD cases.

Functional changes in both cerebral blood flow and metabolism have been shown using positron emission tomography (PET) and SPECT. The literature has been consistent in showing reductions in cerebral blood flow (PET and SPECT studies) and cerebral glucose metabolism (PET) in the temporal/parietal (T/P) cortex. This latter finding corresponds to the extensive neuropathologic changes found in patients with AD (Tomlinson, 1989). Most studies have found significant relationships between these T/P changes and the degree of cognitive impairment (Haxby et al., 1986; Dekosky et al., 1990).

Of these two methods, SPECT is much cheaper and more widely available to practicing physicians. SPECT scans, primarily using the radiotracers Tc99m-HMPAO and 123-IMP, are useful in confirming the diagnosis in AD patients with moderate to severe dementia. The diagnostic accuracy of spect in a large number of studies has varied from 85 to 100 percent, with more recent studies showing greater accuracy. The major findings are bilateral decreases in cerebral blood flow in the temporal parietal areas. In most studies the extent of these blood flow abnormalities correlates with severity of disease. Perhaps the greatest potential for SPECT lies in two as yet poorly investigated areas. The first is in the identification of mild cases of AD and related diseases. Most published studies have looked at moderate to severe cases. It is the early detection that would be most useful, especially for drug treatment protocols targeted at arresting the progression of disease. The second use may be in the diagnosis of "mixed disease"—cases where AD and stroke occur together. This is beginning to be recognized as a significant clinical problem, and there are few diagnostic tools available to help in characterizing it.

Interestingly, recent studies have attempted to combine data from two or more of these scanning methods, with the hope that this will provide more information and improve diagnostic accuracy (Fazekas et al., 1989; Pearlson et al., 1992). When Pearlson et al. (1992) combined structural MRI data (cerebral volume measures from the left amygdala and entorhinal cortex—two regions known to be extensively involved in AD) and SPECT data (especially cerebral blood flow measurements from the left temporal/parietal regions), they were able to identify nine patients with the clinical diagnosis of AD from eight controls, with 100 percent discrimination. While this is an early finding, and it must be repeated by other groups in order to become clinically useful, the accuracy reported by this group is quite exciting.

In summary, the neuroimaging findings presented here represent exciting developments in a rapidly evolving field. MRI and SPECT data were targeted, largely because they have the greatest possibility of widespread use by clinicians. More needs to be done, particularly in the identification of milder cases of AD and in the characterization of difficult clinical cases (e.g., "mixed disease"). So far, the results have been encouraging.

References

Bondareff W. et al., 1990. "Magnetic Resonance Imaging and the Severity of Dementia in Older Adults." *Archives of General Psychiatry* 47: 47–51.

Dekosky S. T. et al., 1990. "Assessing Utility of Single Photon Emission Computed Tomography (SPECT) Scan in Alzheimer Disease: Correlation with Cognitive Severity." *Alzheimer Disease Association Disorder* 4: 14–23

Fazekas F. et al., 1989. "Comparison of CT, MR, and PET in Alzheimer's Dementia and Normal Aging." *Journal of Nuclear Medicine* 30: 1607–15.

Haxby J. V. et al., 1986. "Neocortical Metabolic Abnormalities Precede Non-Memory Cognitive Defects in Early Alzheimer's-Type Dementia." *Archives of Neurology* 43: 882–85.

Pearlson G. D. et al., 1992. "Quantitative Changes in Mesial Temporal Volume, Regional Cerebral Blood Flow, and Cognition in Alzheimer's Disease." *Archives of General Psychiatry* 49: 402–8.

Seab J. P. et al., 1988. "Quantitative NMR Measurements of Hippocampal Atrophy in Alzheimer's Disease." *Magnetic Resonance Medicine* 8: 200–208.

Tomlinson B. E., 1989. "The Neuropathology of Alzheimer's Disease— Issues in Need of Resolution." Second Dorothy S. Russell Memorial Lecture. *Neuropathology and Applied Neurobiology* 15: 491–512.

The Coalition on Mental Health and Aging

Larry D. Rickards

The Coalition on Mental Health and Aging was formed in 1991 to provide a forum for aging, mental health, consumer, family, and professional associations and government agencies to work together to improve the quality and accessibility of mental health preventive and treatment services to older persons and their families. More than 30 organizations have joined together to focus on education, services, research, and increased public awareness about the mental health needs of the aged.

The groundwork for the coalition was laid by the American Association of Retired Persons (AARP). Before the first coalition meeting, structured interviews were conducted with staff of associations and government agencies interested in mental health, aging, and research to determine the central issues that need to be addressed. The positive response to the interviews suggested that the time was right to form a coalition.

The information obtained from the interviews clustered into three main areas of concern: the general public's belief that older people do not need or benefit from mental health services; the negative attitude of older people about mental health/illness and their lack of awareness of treatment efficacy; and professional bias against providing mental health services to older people. The first coalition meeting focused discussion on these concerns and how they could be collectively addressed. The first meeting generated dozens of recommendations for the coalition. The task of winnowing these to form a list of achievable objectives was given to a smaller working group, open to all who wished to participate.

In reviewing the recommendations, the working group found many commonalities and overlapping themes. The following central themes emerged: The coalition should: (1) develop an educational approach, (2) address the issue of stigma as it pertains to aging and to mental health, (3) focus on the distinction between normal aging and illness/disease processes, (4) use the media to change ideas, (5) mainstream mental health and aging through all coalition members, and (6) encourage each organization to use its newsletters and other publications to educate its membership.

Three task forces, Consumer Education and the Media, Education of Decision Makers, and Professional Education, were formed to develop projects to advance these themes. The full coalition meets three times a year to review task force proposals and activities, obtain the knowledge and support of individual member organizations for projects, and facilitate networking among participants. The thrust of the coalition is fostering cooperation among coalition members and initiating projects to which members are willing to commit time and effort. AARP continues to provide staff and logistical support.

The coalition has already had remarkable success in four areas. First, the establishment of the Coalition on Mental Health and Aging maintains the active participation of a broad spectrum of national and local organizations. Second, the coalition has actively encouraged and supported the efforts of member organizations in mental health and aging. Examples include providing review and comments to the American Psychological Association in their development of a video to inform older people about the benefits of mental health services, working with the American Medical Association in developing grant solicitations to improve the training of physicians in geriatric mental health and treatment needs, and providing assistance to the National Association of State Mental Health Program Directors in their efforts to replicate mental health and aging coalitions at the state level. Third, in the area of public education, the coalition developed the "Tell the Truth" campaign and held a press briefing to provide national and local media with accurate information about the mental health needs of older people, the warning signs of possible mental health problems, and resource contacts and themes for referrals and future articles. Articles have been developed for member organizations to include in their internal publications. Finally, the coalition has supported professional and national meetings. Its cosponsorship of the special program "Aging and the Emerging Spirit" for the American Society on Aging's 1992 Annual Meeting is an example.

The coalition is looking toward several future activities. Plans are being made to hold a Capitol Hill forum early in the 103rd Congress to educate new and returning members and staff on mental health and aging. The coalition is collaborating with the Federal Council on Aging in revising and updating its publication, *Mental Health and the Elderly*. Other activities will focus on professional education and training and on developing additional articles for the media.

S *Springer Publishing Company*

RETIREMENT COUNSELING
A Handbook for Gerontology Practitioners

Virginia E. Richardson, PhD

With the steadily increasing number of individuals approaching retirement age, many more will require counseling to cope with both the social and economic problems that arise, both in pre- and post-retirement. This book is intended to increase the practitioner's awareness of such problems and to recommend intervention strategies for dealing with them.

Richardson addresses social factors that affect the retirement experience such as gender, ethnic background, and poverty, and offers an integration of theory and practice about retirement as well as a unique conceptualization of retirement problems. This book is invaluable to psychologists, social workers, career and retirement counselors, and any clinician working with older adults.

Contents:

Springer Series on Life Styles and Issues in Aging

1993   224pp   0-8261-7020-X   hardcover

536 Broadway, New York, NY 10012-3955 • (212) 431-4370 • Fax (212) 941-7842

Springer Publishing Company

STRATEGIES FOR THERAPY WITH THE ELDERLY
Living with Hope and Meaning

Claire M. Brody, PhD, and **Vicki G. Semel,** PsyD
with a Foreword by **Margot Tallmer,** PhD

This comprehensive volume provides therapy techniques for mental health professionals who work with the elderly. It is also a pragmatic guide for establishing programs and conducting therapy groups in various health settings.

The book covers three major arenas of psychotherapy with the elderly: therapy with people living in nursing homes, with those living in semi-independent housing and participating in community-oriented activities, and with people living independently and seen in private practice. The book's theme is that meaningful therapy can be accomplished with an aging / elderly population in any setting. Stereotypes about aging are confronted with examples of maturation and change through psychotherapy, both individually and in groups.

Contents

1993   200pp   0-8261-8010-8   hardcover

536 Broadway, New York, NY 10012-3955 • (212) 431-4370 • Fax (212) 941-7842

⑤ Springer Publishing Company

PREVENTING ELDERLY SUICIDE
Overcoming Personal Despair, Professional Neglect, and Social Bias

Joseph Richman, PhD

The elderly have the highest suicide rate of any population group. Richman tackles the problem of suicide in the final stages of life, offering reasons to help explain the phenomenon, as well as responses to various issues. Throughout the book, he advocates therapies most suited to particular cases, rather than a specific kind of therapy.

Richman speaks from experience. For 45 years, he has helped elderly people combat depression, and in that length of time, he has seen thousands of people regain a thirst for life after being down. The mental health professional says he has learned one simple fact: "by and large, depressed, old people get better."

Partial Contents:

I. Demography and the Theoretical Foundations of Elderly Suicide • Danger Signs and Recovery Factors • Family Risk Factors

II. Assessment and Early Intervention • Recognition of the Problem • Assessment and Testing

III. Crisis Intervention • An Outline of Crisis Intervention • The Effect of Past Crises • The Many Faces of Psychiatric Crises

IV. Therapy: The Healing Relationship

V. Family Tensions and Suicide

VI. Group Psychotherapy with Suicidal Patients • The Healing Power of Groups

VII. Individual Psychotherapy • Homage to the Individual

Springer Series on Death and Suicide
1993   224pp   0-8261-7480-9   hardcover

536 Broadway, New York, NY 10012-3955 • (212) 431-4370 • Fax (212) 941-7842